Strangers & Aliens

A Christian Science Fiction Author Examines the
Evidence for Extraterrestrial Life

Tony Breeden

Copyright © 2016 Tony Breeden
All rights reserved.

DEDICATION

This book is dedicated to my wonderful wife, Angela, to my amazing boys, and to all of the teachers and librarians who encouraged me to be weirdly me.

TABLE OF CONTENTS

	Foreword	i
1	Hardwired for Wonder	1
2	The Truth is Fantastic!	11
3	Future Worlds	31
4	Evolution and Science Fiction	47
5	Chasing the Flying Saucers	61
6	Look to the Skies!	81
7	Trust No One	99
8	Unidentified Lying Saucers	127
9	Saucerian Psychology	149
10	It's All the Devil Anyway	179
11	UFOs and the Bible	219
12	Are We Alone?	229
13	Angels and Aliens	259
14	Can Aliens Be Saved?	277
15	The Truth Is Out There	307
	About the Author	317

ACKNOWLEDGMENTS

There are so many people to thank who helped with the writing and research of this book.

Among those who extraordinarily lent their support, knowledge, and expertise are Tim Chaffey, for his insights into Genesis; Syd Edwards, not only for being the former "Godfather of MIDIAN," but for providing me with a report on the Mantell crash; David Houchin, curator of the Gray Barker Collection, for his expertise concerning all things Gray Barker; Mark Opsasnick, for information regarding John Keel and Tom Monteleone; and the amazingly patient staff at the Kanawha County Public Libraries, for helping me tracking down that rare edition of the *Mothman Prophecies*.

Foreword

Before I begin, I would like to take a moment to state what this book is NOT about. I am not trying to prove alien life exists. I actually doubt that it does. I am not trying to say that Christians – or anyone else for that matter – ought to start saying that extraterrestrials exist. If that is what you're looking for, you may as well read something else.

The primary purpose of this book is to caution folks, especially my fellow Biblical creationists, against making dogmatic statements about things the Bible is silent upon and to show that there's really no cause for Christianity to fear the idea of aliens. In fact, the typical objections one encounters are both fallacious and ill-advised.

A secondary purpose of this book is to answer objections to speculative fiction, particularly science fiction, and demonstrate its worth as an exploratory apologetic and/or a meaningful discourse on the shape of the future in which Christians should be informed participants.

Part 1: Science Fiction as Anticipatory Apologetic

1 Hard-Wired for Wonder

During the writing of this book, I took a trip to Blackwater Falls State Park in Davis, West Virginia. It's a place of wondrous natural beauty. In fact, it's one of the most photographed places in the Mountain State. One of the things that really struck me about the experience, amid thick forests carpeted in ferns and the park's namesake thundering waterfall, were the myriad stars visible from the back porch of our cabin that night. The heavens truly declare the glory of God!

It's impossible to look up at such star-kissed heavens without wondering what's out there beyond our bright blue world. Are we alone? Is there life beyond this planet? Is our alien counterpart, some green or gray little man, wondering the very same thing from his homeworld in a galaxy far, far away? Will we ever meet? Or are they already here?

Christian believers are forced to ponder the added questions of, well, Can they be saved? If they can, would Christ have to die on each alien world for their redemption? Does the Bible even allow the possibility of extraterrestrial life? What would it mean for Christianity if intelligent alien life were discovered?

In the summer of 2014, the internet exploded with headlines that Ken Ham of Answers in Genesis, the creationist organization responsible for the Creation Museum and the Ark Encounter in Kentucky, was saying that there was no point in looking for aliens because they were going to hell anyway!

That's not quite what he said, of course. At least, it's not what he meant to say!

Before we go any further, it should be noted that concerns about the salvation of extraterrestrials and other matters of what we call exotheology aren't limited to creationist circles. Catholic astronomer Guy Consolmagno, who dismisses creationism as "a kind of paganism[1]," has written a book called, *Would You Baptize an Extraterrestrial? ...and Other Questions from the Astronomer's Inbox at the Vatican Observatory.* Incidentally, his answer is "Yes, but only if she asks!"

In any case, Ken Ham doesn't even believe intelligent extraterrestrials are even possible, much less going to hell[2]. The reason his opponents ran with the whole "Ken Ham says aliens are going to hell!" business is because he argued his case incompletely[3,4].

On a Creation Today podcast[5] which aired October 14, 2011, Paul Taylor provided a brief summary of the rest of the typical creationist argument against extraterrestrials when he stated that:

> "..the Bible makes it very clear that the earth is the center of man's, of God's intentions. It's the earth that God formed to be inhabited. That's what we read in Isaiah. And you know in many ways, theologically it would be very difficult to believe in aliens elsewhere."

> "I mean how could you do so? How could you believe that God had made the universe, and that the universe was destroyed if you like, marred by the sin of Adam, and that affects the whole universe, so it affects the alien races who presumably didn't sin at that particular point. So it doesn't make sense. But to the evolutionist it makes sense, because they believe life is evolved by chance. If it's evolved by chance on earth, then it could've evolved by chance anywhere in the universe. So it really is an argument about creation and evolution."

So Taylor placed the argument in terms of evolution versus creationism. He based his premise on a common theme in Christian circles: the truism that our starting points determine our views on various subjects.

Ken Ham weighs in similarly:

> "Aliens? Depends on Your Starting Point. Why do so many researchers and scientists believe so strongly that there are aliens out there..? ...[I]t's because of their evolutionary starting point. Starting from God's Word, we have good reasons to reject the idea of intelligent extraterrestrial life and to doubt even the presence of microbial life on other planets[6]."

The trouble is that he presents a false dichotomy: an evolutionary starting point leads to a belief in extraterrestrial life, while, in his words, "from a biblical perspective, we don't expect to find alien life." Certainly on the surface. The battle lines appear to be drawn between creationists who oppose the idea of alien life and evolutionists, Christian or otherwise, who embrace the possibility.

And then there are folks like me.

I'm a creationist who writes science fiction. And I believe in the possibility of intelligent alien life. It's fair to ask why I differ from some of my fellow creationists on the subject.

The simplest answer is that I was hard-wired for wonder.

I was one of those kids with an incredibly overactive imagination. Whether I was listening to the story of two poor children outwitting a cannibal witch in an improbable house made of confectionaries, the tale of God parting the Red Sea for Moses, or the legend of how Robin Hood won the golden arrow, I was left with a sense of wonder. And a hunger for more.

I grew up in West Virginia (mostly), which is admittedly earthbound and Calvinistic for the biggest part, but my family moved up and down the East Coast a lot. I went to sixteen different schools from Kindergarten to 12th grade, if that gives you any idea how much we pulled up stakes. So I grew up amongst snow-covered mountains and warm, pristine beaches. I loved the open road and the adventure that called from the horizon. But I always thought of West Virginia as my home.

Imagination played a big part in my childhood. Since we did move a lot, friends and neighborhoods changed constantly. As a result, I grew up with two brothers who were my worst enemies and best friends all rolled into one. Together, we went on noble quests to slay dragons, free planets from the evil Empire and to bring treasure back from lost cities in the jungle. Fed on a diet of action movies and Saturday morning cartoons, our imaginations knew no limits... at least until simple physics and minor injuries taught us better. One of the other benefits of our unintentionally nomadic lifestyle is that I've probably been to Disney World more times than any kid has a right to. It should come as no surprise that I was fascinated by Walt Disney. I even fancied becoming an animator at one point.

Some of the best movies ever made came out of my childhood years. And some of the worst. My dad and I had little in common, except love for each other and our love for fantasy and science fiction, but I clearly recall watching the original *Star Trek* series on TV and going to see *Return of the Jedi* and *Clash of the Titans* on the big screen with him. I grew up watching movies by Spielberg before he lost his optimism, Lucas before he lost the art of storytelling and Harryhausen before his work was replaced by CGI. Special effects pioneers Harryhausen and John Dykstra were my heroes; in fact, I give them both a more than obvious nod in my second novel, *Luckbane*[7].

I grew up under parents and teachers who encouraged my appetite for books. Yes, literacy was encouraged in West Virginia, my friend! My 5th grade teacher recognized my penchant for the weird and, for better or worse, she indulged (and I daresay encouraged) it by allowing me to give my weekly oral report on anything I found interesting. What I found interesting turned out to be things like piranha, dinosaurs, bats, Bigfoot, Nessie, Walt Disney, flying saucers and anything else that was a bit weird or wonderful. I was a natural born Fortean, but I had no idea who Charles Fort even was! So it's probably little wonder that I've always been drawn to science fiction.

When my imagination needed free fuel, my library card was a precious key to magical realms and adventures far beyond the stars. Eventually I began writing my own stories.

My first serious attempt at writing was science fiction: a space story. I went through several different versions of that space story, but they were all very early Spielberg in tone. Basically, I was abducted by aliens (minus the probes!), who thought I was someone else, someone important even! I was a geek who was frequently bullied in real life, but in my sci-fi tale I was a famous amnesiac who had friends, a potential alien girlfriend, a mechanical helper that was vaguely reminiscent of R2-D2 or the robots from Disney's *The Black Hole*, and a wicked cool spaceship whose command module separated from the rest of the ship when it was needed in a fight. I thought of that latter concept long before I ever saw *Star Trek: The Next Generation*; I was a little put off that someone else "beat me to the idea," as it were.

In high school, that space story became "The Misadventures of Spaceman Sam[8]", one of the several stories that made up the book I called *Bantamwood Tales*. By then, my protagonist's world had been fully developed into an entire universe of creatures and characters, thanks in no small part to a worldbuilding exercise I conducted every day in 11th

Grade English. I was writing a travelogue of sorts. Basically, I would draw some crazy-looking alien and would then proceed to tell you where it came from, what it ate, its basic ecology, what kind of society it had, and all that. It was called *Space Nitwits, or the Book of 100 Characters* and, yes, I did manage to come up with that many. What else was there to do in 11th Grade English when the class was basically 9th Grade English regurgitated, right?

I said all of that to say this: I'm willing to bet that a lot of what I just related resonates with some of you reading this book, especially if you were hard-wired the way I am. If you're not, at least you know where I'm coming from now. Now let's fast forward through this backstory garbage and get to the good stuff!

Once upon a time, a fellow who was hard-wired for wonder wrote a book called *Johnny Came Home*, a sci-fi novel about people who develop super powers in a fictional town in West Virginia. The original cover of the book featured a crashed flying saucer parked in the shadow of a church steeple. The book explores where these people got their powers and I wanted to throw in a red herring of sorts, an implication that they might be extraterrestrial in origin. It wasn't completely misleading; the saucer is in the book, but there are no aliens.

That didn't keep folks from asking me about my views on little green men! Especially after they found out that I was both a preacher and a science fiction author. A lot of folks were under the misapprehension that these two occupations were mutually exclusive[9]. At some point, I realized that I needed to investigate the whole UFO question a bit more if I was going to give anything resembling an intelligent response. (Crazy, right?)

So I started writing and researching this book. I found that I did not quite agree with my fellow apologists on the question of the possibility of extraterrestrial life and its implications on theology.

***

Notes

1. "Creationism dismissed as 'a kind of paganism' by Vatican's astronomer." *The Scotsman Newspaper.* May 5, 2006. Scotsman.com. Web. Retrieved April 26, 2016.

2. Ham, Ken. "Are aliens going to hell?" July 29, 2014. AnswersinGenesis.org. Retrieved April 14, 2016.

3. Ham, Ken. "We'll find a new earth within 20 years." July 20, 2014. AnswersinGenesis.org. Retrieved April 14, 2016.

4. Well... in that article anyway. To be fair, Ken Ham has an entire website dedicated to expounding his position, but apparently no one could be bothered to see if they were quoting him in context.

5. "Did a giant asteroid kill off the dinosaurs?"

Creation Today. October 14, 2011. Podcast. Transcript. Accessed April 20, 2016.

6. Ham, Ken. "Will Aliens Contact the Earth in 1500 Years?" July 2, 2016. AnswersinGenesis.org. Retrieved July 13, 2016.

7. In *Luckbane*, the first book in my Otherworld series, there is a war wizard named Throm of Dykstra. The wizard's truename is Raymundo Harryhausen. I only hope my readers find it a fitting tribute to two of cinema's finest technowizards!

8. I freely admit the title was derivative of Calvin & Hobbes' Spaceman Spiff. In my opinion, Bill Waterson is a genius to have so evocatively captured the essence of every boy's daydream double lives.

9. I've had more than one review that mentions how the reviewer supposed that Christian sci-fi author was an oxymoron until they read one of my books.

2 The Truth is Fantastic!

Like many folks of my generation[1], I freely admit that I rebelled against the church and went the whole prodigal route. Basically, when I graduated from high school, I graduated from church as well. Some folks assume that my penchant for dragons and Daleks and other general weirdness contributed to that decision to leave. If anything, it was actually quite the opposite. While my reasons for leaving were varied, one of the bigger ones concerned how the Church tends to deal with creativity.

I'll just spell it out for you. For those of us whom God has hard-wired for wonder, the church can often be more of a hindrance to artistic imagination than a help. Certainly, conservative Christianity has not always embraced creativity. For example, when I was a teenager in a Baptistic Christian school, I was told that I couldn't draw a T-rex because the teacher thought it looked demonic. I'll admit that tyrannosaurs are scary-looking (it's the teeth!), but not everything that looks scaly and predatory is a demon, y'all. My well-meaning teacher wasn't really sure what to do with a creative young mind who was obsessed with dinosaurs and dragons, so she did what a lot of Christians and churches do when faced with such things: she banned it.

The irony is that now creationist organizations are actively seeking talented artists who can realistically render a toothsome "terrible lizard."

Even if this weren't the case, I can't help thinking

our Creator, the paragon and fountainhead of creativity, meant us to be so much more. Yet if Christians are called to walk "in His steps," why aren't churches at the vanguard of creativity? Why does the introduction of new music into the church service produce civil warfare rather than encouragement of the musicians' expression of praise and worship? Why is a lot of religious artwork so predictable?

Especially when you consider that, first and foremost, the Bible is a book of Wonders, which is little wonder (pun intended) if you stop to consider how very creative its Chief Author is. The Bible contains records of supernatural miracles and prophecies to inspire awe and wonder of God in those who read its stories. The God we serve created the heavens and the earth and all that is in them in six short days … and even had time at the end of each day to appreciate His own handiwork and place His personal stamp of approval on it. When we look at the night sky through a telescope or at the incredibly tiny worlds captured between the slides of a microscope, we see the level of detail and grandeur of which the ultimate Creative Type is capable of. We admire Tolkien for the influence his work as a linguist had upon his stories, but it was God who spoke first, and who first imagined not only human language, but whale and bird song and the dancing language of bees.

When the Creator came to this earth, He certainly preached; however, the Master Teacher also chose creative teaching stories (parables) to get His points across. You see, stories, like songs, tend to stick with you, making their lessons easy to recall and to generalize to our particular situation. Maybe that's why much of the inspired Word of God is broken down into stories. The Author and the Editor of our faith can certainly be counted on to know a thing or two about the art of effective storytelling!

Some of my fellow Christian apologists disparage this tendency to look at the Bible's history in terms of stories. There's concern that we learn history in school, but mere Bible stories in church, diminishing the influence of Scriptural truth in our children's lives. I've fallen off of this particular bandwagon. You see, as a storyteller I've come to realize that the power of the Gospel is in the fact that it is the Greatest Story Ever Told. The Bible is what we call a True Myth. By myth, I do not mean a story that is not true; in the academic sense, a myth is "a story that serves to define the fundamental worldview of a culture by explaining aspects of the natural world and delineating the psychological and social practices and ideals of a society[2]." So by True Myth, I mean a story that can shape cultures and change lives which also happens to be historically true.

Evolutionists are only just realizing the power of the story. Michael Dowd and his wife Connie Barlow style themselves as "evolution evangelists." One of the things they've begun to promote is what they call "The Great Story." Also known as the Universe Story, Epic of Evolution, or Big History, the Great

Story is, according to the couple's website, "humanity's common creation story… a sacred narrative of an evolving Universe of emergent complexity and breathtaking creativity — a story that offers each of us the opportunity to find meaning and purpose in our lives and our time in history[3]."

They have the Great Story, but we still have the Greatest Story Ever Told, and ours makes a great deal more sense to the reader. The "Great Story" lacks a point. I mean, we're really supposed to find meaning and purpose in something that, if true, is indifferent, undirected, pitiless, meaningless and blind?? They say that we must make our own meaning, but what that really means is that we must make-believe that anything has meaning at all! Such a worldview is an empty box wrapped in bright promises. As dear Mr. Tumnus would say, "always winter and never Christmas."

In any case, my point is that we don't really have to choose between Biblical history and Bible stories – it's preferable that we don't!

Now when this old prodigal came back to the fold, I ran into a little problem. As I said, I was hard-wired for wonder, but the Christian speculative fiction scene was almost non-existent. What was a natural-born geek in God's pasture to do?

By this point, my writing was sort of a half-forgotten hobby. My decision to start writing seriously came as a direct result of browsing the near-exclusive sea of Amish/romance novels of the local Christian bookstores. I remember thinking, Why should I be forced to get the stuff I actually enjoy reading from secular bookstores in novels written from a non- or even anti-Christian worldview? What about the stuff of traditional sci-fi? What about alien worlds? Aliens? Space travel? Artificial Intelligence? Where was the Christian exploration of these subjects? In essence, why couldn't I read "Do Android Prayers Reach the Ears of God?" in the tradition of "Do Androids Dream of Electric Sheep?"(the inspiration for the movie *Blade Runner)*?

The success of the *Left Behind* book series demonstrated how influential exploratory fiction could be in shaping and reinforcing beliefs concerning eschatology. I realized that apologetics fiction could do the same for evangelical convictions concerning our origins. With that in mind, I set out to tell a great sci-fi story that gave a plausible young earth creationist explanation of comic book super powers rather than the prevalent evolutionary assumption of beneficial mutations, popularized in the *X-Men* movies and on TV shows like *Heroes*, *No Ordinary Family*, *The Tomorrow People* and *Alphas*. As I mentioned, the result of that endeavor was *Johnny Came Home*, a book about a young man who returns to the town of his birth to uncover the truth of why he can do things no one's ever seen outside of movies and comic books.

I've come to realize that, despite my personal preference for speculative fiction, the science fiction and fantasy genres are a bit of a hard sell for the traditional Christian book market and, perhaps as a result, for Christianity-at-large.

In a much cited article that first appeared in the *Journal of Creation* 15, no. 2 (Aug 2001; pp.81-88), with the heavy-handed title, "Science fiction: a Biblical perspective[4]," Christian apologist David J. Laughlin criticized science fiction as being "permeated with unrealism, humanism, occultism, New Age philosophy, Eastern mysticism and evolutionism."

Speculative fiction critic E. Franz Rottersteiner has lamented that 'the "science" of science fiction is often indistinguishable from magic,[5]" but perhaps this is no surprise in light of the third and best known of British sci-fi author Arthur C. Clarke's Laws: "Any sufficiently advanced technology is indistinguishable from magic."

The fact that science fiction often employs what might be termed "unrealism" in regards to things like faster than light travel, disintegration rays, alien species from different worlds being able to interbreed with impunity, et cetera, has been cited as a criticism of the genre by Christians and non-Christians alike. The charge of unrealism is not altogether unjustified, but, at the same time, neither is it necessarily damning to the genre. I mean, it is *fiction*, after all.

The reason why science fiction tends to be more speculation than science is because we're telling stories. Science fiction's Hugo awards are named for Hugo Gernsback. Gernsback's formula for the perfect science fiction story was "75 percent literature interwoven with 25 percent science." This formula, or rather the premise behind this formula, is what allows science fiction to inspire curiosity and shape our beliefs. In short, science fiction is the thinking man's genre. A recognition of this fact led West Virginia House Representative Ray Canterbury to introduce H. R. 2983, a 2013 bill intended to require "inclusion of science fiction reading material in certain existing middle school and high school courses to stimulate interest in the fields of math and science." In other words, he intended to make science fiction compulsory reading in West Virginia's secondary schools. As of the publication of this book, the bill languishes in committee.

Science fiction doesn't just affect our views on science because our "What if?" questions aren't simply concerned with science alone. Science fiction also asks questions about the future of recreation, morality, religion, politics, culture, and more. For example, I mentioned how the *Left Behind* series demonstrated how influential exploratory fiction could be in shaping and reinforcing beliefs concerning eschatology. A reader comes away from Veronica Roth's *Divergent* (2011) series convinced that socialism is just wrong. We are reminded that some things are worth fighting for and not to be placated by a corrupt government's offer of free bread and bloody entertainment as we read Suzanne Collins' *Hunger Games* (2008) series. Indeed, the series' dystopian allusions to the violence and decadence of the Roman Empire serve as a tacit warning that we should be careful not to allow the past to be repeated!

If I were to be fair, I would note that, in general, the Christian fiction market has a problem of unrealism.

One of the major reasons for this problem is the unofficial but still very real Christian fiction standards most commonly associated with publishers affiliated with the Christian Bookselling Association (CBA) and the Evangelical Christian Publisher's Association (ECPA).

I personally don't hold to those standards, but before I tell you why, let's loosely define the sort of standards I'm talking about. Christian fiction of the CBA/ECPA stripe may be defined as fiction that has the three following three criteria[6]:

> 1 – The author avoids the use of graphic sex/violence and foul language.
>
> 2 – The story is based on Biblical teachings and/or conveys or reflects the author's Christian beliefs/worldview.
>
> 3 – The author is a Christian.

The reason I reject the CBA/ECPA standards is because of that first criterion. Keep in mind that these standards are well-intentioned; they were born of a desire to provide a safe alternative to non-Christian fiction. So this might sound like an odd thing to say, but as a preacher, that sends up a red flag.

Hebrews 5:11-14 says:

> "Of whom we have many things to say, and hard to be uttered, seeing ye are dull of hearing. For when for the time ye ought to be teachers, ye have need that one teach you again which be the first principles of the oracles of God; and are become such as have need of milk, and not of strong meat. For every one that useth milk is unskilful in the word of righteousness: for he is a babe. But strong meat belongeth to them that are of full age, even those who by reason of use have their senses exercised to discern both good and evil."

The basic idea is that we mature as Christians by exercising discernment. We're supposed to walk instead of crawl at some point. We're supposed to leave our tricycles and big wheels behind for bicycles when the time is right. The training wheels are supposed to come off at some point. You get the idea. The CBA/ECPA standards are meant to eliminate the need for discernment.

That first criterion is usually extended to prohibit all potentially objectionable things like ghosts, vampires, zombies, extraterrestrials, superpowers, magic, *et cetera, ad nauseam*. Of course, this means that very little traditional speculative fiction gets published by those adhering to CBA/ECLA related standards, right? You see, the entire purpose of that criterion is to assure Christian readers that these Christian books are safe, so there's a bit of overkill at play, to say the least.

Which leads me to my other, more visceral reason for rejecting those arbitrary standards: that white gloved first criterion can also be used to condemn portions of the Bible that contain the sorts of things they don't allow in Christian fiction. Personally, I tire of Christian fiction which seeks to be cleaner than my Bible. My Bible includes violence, witchcraft, substance abuse, swearing, idolatry, and sexual sin. It is in parts graphic (read the last few chapters of Judges if you doubt me) and even explicit (or haven't you read the Song of Songs lately?) I also tire of the Christian fiction industry's insistence that were sterilize our fiction to the point where we would be forced to condemn the Good Book by the self-same standard if we weren't being arbitrary. Any literary standard which could, if applied consistently and non-arbitrarily, condemn the Bible should be eschewed by Christians.

Nevertheless, Laughlin warned that:

> "When concepts are built from unrealities, the end result is an elaborate system of fabrication that is as sturdy as a house built on

> sand (Matthew 7:26–27). What value can such a system offer the real world? How edifying can a scheme of impossibilities be, however impressive or clever its presentation?"

He was wrong on all counts. Fairy tales and fables edify despite being entirely unrealistic. Prophetic dreams and visions filled with such unrealities as skeletons coming to life, many-winged leopards and carnivorous cows edify as well. Like Laughlin, C.S. Lewis famously argued that myths were "lies and therefore worthless, even though breathed through silver," until Tolkien showed him the error of his ways. Something need not be entirely chained to reality in order to edify. And to be fair, the Bible is full of things that Christians accept as reality that secularists would classify as unrealities: talking snakes and donkeys, divine messengers and messages, and men rising from the dead being chief among them.

Science fiction has a lot in common with futurism (aka futurology or future studies). Futurism is a branch of social science that attempts to predict possible, probable, and preferable futures and the beliefs and worldviews that underlie them. In the introduction to *The Left Hand of Darkness*, Ursula K. LeGuin said that futurism is the business of prophets, clairvoyants and futurists, while, in contrast, "a novelist's business is lying;" however, I think this distinction ignores the fact that many novelists are in fact futurists because the process of credible world building requires us to think like a futurist.

Hugo Gernsback was the publisher of *Amazing Stories*, the first science fiction magazine, and was also the man who coined the term science fiction (although he preferred to use the term "scientifiction"). Gernsback wrote the following the very first issue of *Amazing Stories* (April 1926):

> "By 'scientifiction,' I mean the Jules Verne, H. G. Wells and Edgar Allan Poe type of story—a charming romance intermingled with scientific fact and prophetic vision."

As science fiction authors, we must often postulate future histories, cultures, innovations, factions, places, and their consequences upon one another. We basically research and develop a future world – sometimes an entire universe – that is believable enough for our reader to be willing to suspend disbelief.

In his essay "On Fairy Stories" (1947), J.R.R. Tolkien wrote that the storyteller became a "successful 'sub-creator'" by making a "Secondary World which your mind can enter. Inside it, what he relates is "true": it accords with the laws of that world. You therefore believe it, while you are, as it were, inside. The moment disbelief arises, the spell is broken; the magic, or rather art, has failed."

To understand what he meant by becoming a sub-creator, we turn to his poem *Mythopoeia* (1931), where he describes the human author as "the little maker" with his "own small golden scepter" lording over his "subcreation" just as God rules over His primary Creation. In other words, worldbuilding is a genuine act of sub-creation. Just as mankind was made in God's image, our sub-creations are a reflection of His primary Creation. More importantly, if worldbuilding is done successfully, those sub-creations, while we are immersed in them, are just as real and genuine as God's primary creation.

The very ability to imagine things that aren't currently realities is part of what makes us human. This ability to visualize things that might be is what makes it possible for us to problem solve and conceive new ideas and technologies. Faster than light travel is currently thought to be impossible; we're simply imagining a future world where those present impossibilities have been overcome by future discoveries.

Of course, Laughlin isn't really harping against unrealities for their own sake. His chief concern in this department is his belief that sci-fi unrealities are evidence of man's rebellion against God. For example, Laughlin condemns science fiction for making space too hospitable because he sees an agenda in doing so. Man has rejected His Creator, "[s]o, he searches elsewhere to fulfil these needs. Maybe, he reasons, outer space has something to offer that cannot be found here. Perhaps the grass is greener on the other side of the galaxy. Consequently, man exalts the heavens. He makes outer space to be far more friendly than it really is. Unfortunately, this results in a misdirected placement of hope. The extravagant and expensive efforts to search for intelligent life in space is an example of this. The Scriptures condemn such glorification of the heavens (Deuteronomy 4:19; Isaiah 47:13–14; Jeremiah 8:1–2)."

Unfortunately, the verses he cites are wildly out-of-context. Those verses warn against consulting and worshipping the stars, not against searching the heavens for signs of extraterrestrial life or planets hospitable to life. Laughlin's statements also betray an ignorance of science fiction that paints space travel as anything but easy. Maybe he should take .the time to watch a few episodes of Joss Whedon's *Firefly* (2002-2003), particularly "Out of Gas," an episode that has the crew of the *Serenity* dealing with harsh lifeor-death decisions due to a disastrous mechanical failure.

In their efforts to demonize science fiction, some folks also tend to misapply verses dealing with the word "imagination" to imply that imagination is evil; however, faith itself, as defined by the Bible, is an act of imagination: Faith is the substance of things hoped for, the evidence of things not seen [Hebrews 11:1]. I'm not implying that God is imaginary; any more than Einstein was saying knowledge was useless when he said, "Imagination is better than knowledge." Imagination is the act of visualizing what is presently not in front of us. All of us use it to some extent, whether we are planning our week, reading a book or creating a musical masterpiece. Imagination is the chief gift God has given us to set us apart from the animals. As Chesterton wrote in the final chapter of *Orthodoxy*[7]:

> "That man and brute are like is, in a sense, a truism; but that being so like they should then be so insanely unlike, that is the shock and the enigma. That an ape has hands is far less interesting to the philosopher than the fact that having hands he does next to nothing with them; does not play knuckle-bones or the violin; does not carve marble or carve mutton. People talk of barbaric architecture and debased art. But elephants do not build colossal temples of ivory even in a roccoco style; camels do not paint even bad pictures, though equipped with the material of many camel's-hair brushes. Certain modern dreamers say that ants and bees have a society superior to ours. They have, indeed, a civilization; but that very truth only reminds us that it is an inferior civilization. Who ever found an ant-hill decorated with

the statues of celebrated ants? Who has seen a bee-hive carved with the images of gorgeous queens of old?"

Unless you're just a Christian opposed to fiction in general, Laughlin's condemnation based on unrealities in fiction isn't likely to hold water; I doubt anyone will ever give me a convincing argument against using fictional stories to convey truth, since Jesus told parables and Nathan the prophet told a story to King David to convince him of his own guilt.

Besides, there is a point to these unrealities. Chesterton said of fairy-stories (or "nursery-tales") that:

> "These tales say that apples were golden only to refresh the forgotten moment when we found that they were green. They make rivers run with wine only to make us remember, for one wild moment, that they run with water[8]."

Though such luminaries as C.S. Lewis and J.R.R. Tolkien blazed the trail for writing speculative fiction from a Christian mythos, today Christian sci-fi and fantasy authors are kind of the black sheep of the evangelical ghetto. We write about aliens and elves, magic and super-powered mutants, things that make some Christians very uncomfortable. I can tell you that Christian sci-fi and fantasy authors take our craft and our faith very seriously. A lot of us see ourselves as exploratory apologists or, more specifically in the case of sci-fi authors, anticipatory apologists. We ponder how technology and future discoveries might impact traditional Christianity because [A] we love a good sci-fi story and [B] it's a great medium to ask the sort of uncomfortable questions that nevertheless allow us to anticipate ways to provide reasonable answers, in the spirit of 2 Peter 3:15.

While I would never devalue the opinion of scientists and theologians regarding exotheology, it would be equally unwise to ignore the input of those whom God has gifted with an abundance of imagination. I don't think anyone outside the fields of writing (and one includes novels, comics and screenwriting in this context) realizes the level of detail and thought that goes into our worldbuilding. We create new technologies, cultures, grammar, entertainment, politics… the list goes on and on. And in the process, a Christian author tends to ask themselves how these proposed changes in the future will affect Christian theology. I dare say, we've considered more than theologians have ever yet dreamt.

Speaking of which…

If I can wax homiletic for a moment, when a Christian speculative fiction author considers the words of Paul recorded in 1 Corinthians 2:9 [referring to Isaiah 64:4] that "Eye hath not seen, nor ear heard, neither have entered into the heart of man, the things which God hath prepared for them that love him," we get reeeally excited because we've imagined so very much, and yet the mystery escapes us!

I owe a great debt to Frank Peretti and C.S. Lewis, who showed us that we could tell great stories, deal with doubts and questions, and encourage others in their Christian faith at the same time. Exploratory fiction also gives Christians a voice into the future that we've largely left to those antagonistic to the faith. In other words, science fiction is often either hostile or ambivalent to Christianity because we let folks with other worldviews dominate the genre and imagineer the future for us — and as a result many folks feel that in some way religion will become increasingly irrelevant!

This is a conversation that Christianity needs to be a part of, because science fiction isn't just about exploring possible futures.

I think Hugo and Nebula award winning author Robert J. Sawyer said it best, when he noted that the sci-fi author's job "is not to predict the future. Rather, it's to suggest all the possible futures — so that society can make informed decisions about where we want to go. George Orwell's science-fiction classic Nineteen Eighty-Four wasn't a failure because the future it predicted failed to come to pass; rather, it was a resounding success because it helped us prevent that future.[9]"

Thankfully, there a lot of great Christian writers, so many others besides myself, a growing movement of what fellow author J.C. Lamont terms "literary apologists," who are creating worlds where we can explore answers to the problems Christianity might face in the future and how the church will look if Christ delays a few more centuries (or more).

Yet when people start asking questions like, "Can aliens be saved?" or, "Would Christ have to die on multiple worlds to save extraterrestrials?" no one ever bothers to ask the very folks who've invested a ton of time and careful thought asking science fiction's "What if?" questions in regards to Christian doctrine.

Therein lies the problem.

***

Notes

1. Generation X, for the record, but, sadly, I've come to find that my spiritual journey transcends generations.

2. Grassie, William. Politics by Other Means: Science and Religion in the Twenty-First Century. XLibris (2010), p. 27.

3. "What is The Great Story?" http://thegreatstory.org/what_is.html. Web. Retrieved 28 February 2016.

4. This article was republished at AnswersinGenesis.org:

https://answersingenesis.org/culture/science-fiction-a-biblical-perspective/.

5. Rottensteiner, E., *The Science Fiction Book*, Seabury Press (1975), p. 8.

6. These criteria are general guidelines for discussion. No list of CBA/ECPA guidelines exists; however, everyone agrees that these criteria exist.

7. Chesterton, G.K., Orthodoxy. John Lane Company (1908), reprinted by Ignatius Press (1995), p. 150-51.

8. *Ibid.*, p. 59.

9. Sawyer, Robert J. "The Purpose of Science Fiction." *Slate*.com. (27 January 2011) http://www.slate.com/articles/technology/future_tense/2011/01/the_purpose_of_science_fiction.html. Accessed 15 September 2016.

3 Future Worlds

The biggest reasons for Christianity's resistance to science fiction is bound up in our views on origins (special creation versus all-natural evolution) and in our eschatology, our beliefs about the End of All Things.

As Paul Legget wrote in an article for *Christianity Today*[1]:

> "The sci-fi tradition thus poses metaphysical- and theological- questions to the ever expanding domain of scientific knowledge. One might view these questions in terms of at least two biblical motifs: Creation and the Fall, and the Apocalypse."

End Times views within Christendom come in a few clearly defined and argued categories. Most folks are familiar with the Darbyist view, aka the Dispensational Premillennial Rapture view, made popular in the 1830s by John Nelson Darby and the Plymouth Brethren and then given wider influence by the publication of the *Scofield Reference Bible* (1909). After *Scofield*, this End Times scenario was then worked out in excruciating detail by Clarence Larkin in a rather mind-blowing series of charts in *Dispensational Truth* (1918), which scenario was popularized even further by Hal Lindsey's *The Late Great Planet Earth* (1970), which even managed to be made into a documentary narrated by Orson

Welles in 1979. *The Late Great Planet Earth* was a precursor to Tim Lahaye and Jerry B. Jenkins' wildly popular *Left Behind* series (1995).

Writing in *The Christian Century* (September 25-October 8, 2002, pp. 8-9), news editor John Hart criticized it as "beam me up theology," but you have to admit it's exciting stuff! A small, desperate, but resolute band of believers beleaguered by the all-powerful Anti-Christ, a megalomaniacal dictator in control of a fascist New World Order. The story has a powerful opening hook: the sudden disappearance of every Bible-believing Christian on the planet. It climaxes in the bona fide War to End All Wars, the Armageddon, and the Triumphant Return of Christ. The setting and the Bible's mention of martyrs and divine judgments make any half-decent effort a gripping read. Once upon a time, I would have said that if Christendom had an established sci-fi market at all, it is predominantly for this specific flavor of End Times fiction.

The trouble is that we have our future so well figured out that no one's allowed to speculate about it. There's no room, seemingly, for space exploration, robot sapience, aliens or anything else that seems to complicate an imminent fulfillment of earth-bound Bible prophecy. If aliens are included in our fiction at all, they're scripted in per Gary Bates' *Alien Intrusion* (2006) or Chuck Missler & Mark Eastman's *Alien Encounters* (1997) as a Satanic deception generally involving some version of the Nephilim of Genesis chapter 6.

For example, Tom Doyle comments on *Nephilim* (1999) by L.A. Marzulli (who admits that his books were greatly influenced by Missler and Eastman) and *We All Fall Down* (2000) by Brian Caldwell in an April 8, 2002 article of *Strange Horizons*[2]:

> "...Christian apocalyptic authors, like science fiction authors, are interested in aliens. But again, they don't like them. Although C.S. Lewis could fit other worlds with sentient beings into his Christian beliefs, this is not the case for the Christian apocalyptic fiction that I've seen. In such works, extraterrestrials are usually just a hoax -- but if they exist, they are actually fallen angels. In *Nephilim*, the demons look just like the greys. In *We All Fall Down*, the demon aliens (called the Celestine Prophets) give a long speech to explain away the Rapture in terms of alien intervention..."

Doyle notes that tendency to give a Satanic origin to technologies and discoveries we find threatening to Christianity, in order to nullify said threat, applies to artificial intelligence and cloning technology as well. For example, he notes that the supercomputer in Marlin Maddoux' *Seal of Gaia* (1998) owes its sentience to the fact that it's demon-possessed. Likewise, cloning Hitler in Robert Van Kampen's

The Fourth Reich (1997) and cloning Christ in both James BeauSeigneur's *Christ Clone Trilogy* (1997-98) and Bill Myer's *Fire of Heaven Trilogy* (1996-99) all result in the AntiChrist.

Some might object that Christian fiction has to be written this way because we know from the Scriptures that this is how things will end. That's certainly the impression that Clarence Larkin's dispensationalist charts give anyway! Of course, the Jews had the Messiah's coming all figured out when they arranged for the crucifixion of Christ, so I tend to be wary of those who think they've got a lock on the future – and End Times Bible scholars *do* think they've got it all figured out! They'll demur that no one knows the day or the hour, but they've nailed the rest of it down – and it's gonna be within the next decade, at least!

I wonder.

If the Lord tarries another millennium or two, what does the Rapture or the Second Coming look like from space? What if we've colonized other worlds as Allan & Aaron Reini's humanity do in *Flight of the Angels* [2012]? Don't tell me it's not possible. Mark 13:27 specifically says that:

> "And then shall he send his angels, and shall gather together his elect from the four winds, from the uttermost part of the earth to the **uttermost part of heaven**" [emphasis mine].

There are three heavens in Scripture. It is generally agreed that the First Heaven is the air we breathe, the atmosphere; the Second Heaven is outer space; and the Third Heaven Paul mentioned in 2 Corinthians 12:2-4 is the abode of God, which in all likelihood exists beyond our universe; which is to say, beyond space-time or, at the very least, beyond the natural world. Since man has breached the First Heaven and begun exploring the Second Heaven Mark 13:27 rationally refers to both the First and Second Heavens. Unless we want to consider the possibility of a believer who misses the Second Coming simply because they chose to be an astronaut or a colonist on Mars.

We may be living in the End Times; there's no way to know for certain. Comedian Mike Warnke used to joke that he could cross-reference Revelation with the evening news, but the prophetic clues were apparently just as imminent to the Apostles. In the meantime, Christian sci-fi authors ask us to consider whether the Bible would still be true if a meteor shattered the planet or the sun went supernova? I mean, is it even Scripturally permissible to consider a universe where Earth is completely destroyed before End Times events in light of Biblical prophecy? Could the speculative apologist possibly imagine a scenario where the Bible's prophecies extend to an Earth 2.0?

If we were to build a time machine and travel 100 years into the future, what would the church look like? Does anyone go to a building anymore or does worship take place in a virtual reality environment? What does faith look like on an alien planet? On a space station? What does post-alien invasion faith look like? Do we still have Orthodox, Catholic and Protestant adherents? Have we merged? Are we more fragmented? Are there all-new denominations and cults to contend with? What do other religions look like? Are the old religions which compete with Christianity still in place or has some new religion like technoGaia-ism taken their place? What does Christian compromise and apostasy look like in the future? Has there been a great falling away from the faith? Are Christians hunted or are they merely marginalized in a sea of new religions and ideologies? Are there exclusively Christian star colonies?

Before you make the mistake of saying that these scenarios are impossible because God would never allow such a thing to happen, know that there were those in my grandfather's generation who similarly boasted that God would not allow us to put a man on the moon because He hadn't allowed man to finish the Tower of Babel. In the eyes of these well-meaning mountain preachers, this whole "man on the moon" business was foolishness and humanism, for the Earth alone was made to be inhabited and the heavens belonged to God Himself. This view was misguided. The fact that the Earth was made to be inhabited did not preclude man from exploring the moon that orbited it.

As for Babel, in Genesis 11:4 we read the boast of those who proposed the Tower's construction:

> "Come, let us build ourselves a city, and a tower whose top is in the heavens; let us make a name for ourselves, lest we be scattered abroad over the face of the whole earth."

God didn't allow man to finish the Tower because we had disobeyed His explicit command to inhabit the entire Earth [Genesis 9:1,7]; instead we were gathered in one place and God saw that disobedient mankind would be able to accomplish whatever evil we set their minds to if we remained united [Genesis 11:6]. It had nothing to do with some imaginary prohibition on reaching the heavens! The lesson of Babel is that God's purpose will not be thwarted by man's will. The lesson of man reaching the moon is that we should never make the mistake of thinking that God will limit our horizons to keep our doctrines as simple as we'd like! In fact, that is the entire point of exploratory apologetics: to anticipate a Christian response to something we currently find implausible but which could come to pass in the future.

That is not to say that there are not definite limitations one must concede when writing about time travel from a Biblical point of view. God knows what will happen, even if some madman in a blue police box isn't quite certain at times, meaning that history is in a sense already written. We may get the details of End Times prophecy wrong so that it happens further in the future than we supposed or whatever, but we can be assured that it will be fulfilled. In other words, prophecy cannot be averted!

Likewise, the idea of going back in time to kill Hitler will never be realized. You can't step on a butterfly in the past and cause America to lose the Revolution. These things are already realized and therefore cannot be changed. Any attempt to alter the timeline could result in something very much like what happened to Balaam, who intended to curse Israel when God had already blessed it. An angel would have slain him if it weren't for the intervention of a beast of burden and a sudden look into the spiritual realm. Balaam ended up further blessing Israel. The point is that if we try to kill Hitler, we stand a good chance of being struck down by an invisible angel. We may want to keep this fact in mind if we ever get the notion in our heads to travel back to the time of Creation. I've little doubt that God would prevent fallen man from entering His very good creation; we may encounter the flaming sword of the angelic guardian of Eden [Genesis 3:24]. Or maybe not. Balaam's intended meddling had already been anticipated by God; if we're able to act in the past or future, we can rest assured that history has already taken our meddling into account and came up with the result recorded in our history books despite our best efforts.

Christian sci-fi authors tend to shy away from an honest-to-goodness aliens take over the world story –

unless we can tie it in to fallen angels and/or a set-up for the End of Days. Folks such as Chuck Missler and Mark Eastman have suggested the End Times will bring with it the return of the Nephilim of Genesis 6 under the guise of being extraterrestrials (or alien half-breeds). As previously mentioned, his concept has spawned Christian sci-fi like L.A. Marzulli's *Nephilim* Trilogy, which has further popularized such scenarios, in the minds of some Christians, as a potentially legitimate alternate eschatology.

To be fair, it is possible that an extraterrestrial deception could be a part of the fulfillment of End Times prophecy. It's not probable, but it is possible.

Let me explain.

UFO true believers who see aliens as future benefactors tend to re-interpret end-times Bible prophecy to one of the two following scenarios:

- "The aliens have been studying us for a long time and in order to save the planet, they will take Christians and anyone else they know will be a hindrance to bringing peace to the planet, saving Mother earth, beginning the next stage of human evolution, or any combination thereof away on their flying saucers and dispose of them for the greater good. This is a counterfeit of the Christian premillennial view where millions of Christians disappear but for all the wrong reasons. Basically, The Rapture becomes proof not that Christians were right about the

Bible all along but that they served a religion that was bad for the planet and so were removed.... According to their own Bible's prophecy?

- Another version of the alien rapture has UFO believers and everyone else who has "spiritually evolved" or received enlightenment leaving the planet at the End of Days, leaving the Earth behind to destroy itself. In other versions, the UFO believers and their enlightened ones are returned to the planet after it has been cleansed and terraformed, which they relate to the Tribulation and subsequent Millennial reign of peace prophesied in Scripture. This is, more or less, the premise of the movie *Knowing* [2009] starring Nicholas Cage, except that the world ends with no possibility of rebirth. Conspicuously, it also features angels as aliens.

The question becomes: Would the Antichrist use the notion of an alien rapture to cover up the real event? Keep in mind that if a pre-Tribulational Rapture occurs and God takes all of the faithful off of this planet in the blink of an eye, one of two things is going to happen. Either [A] a LOT of people are going to vanish from this planet instantly, causing all sorts of mayhem as cars and other vehicles are left driverless, people run around looking for their loved ones, and all that (i.e., the classic scenario); or [B] such a great falling away [2 Thessalonians 2:3] has occurred that only a handful of people vanish and almost no one notices, leaving practically nothing to explain (i.e., the scenario no one likes to think about). Obviously, no one needs an alien angle for the latter scenario, but what about that first one?

Frankly, the level of mayhem and terror the classic Rapture would cause is difficult to fathom. The *Left Behind* books did a decent job of describing the effects of the instant departure of millions of believers. By contrast, in the *Left Behind* movies, the Rapture seems to consist of panic-inducing sets of folded clothes and a few fender benders. Even the most recent cinematic incarnation of *Left Behind* [2014] starring, once again, Nicholas Cage, is little more than an airplane disaster movie.

Let's just say it would be really, really bad and the world would demand answers. Now the irony is that the classic Rapture, even though it's an extremely dramatic fulfillment of Biblical prophecy, does not convince the world to turn to God. Rather, the Bible says that because the world refused the truth before the Rapture, God sends a strong delusion that the world may believe the lie [2 Thessalonians 2:11]. Some of the folks who investigate the sort of things the alleged aliens have said about the Rapture suggest that we're being groomed to believe a big lie. Perhaps this Rapture cover up is the entire purpose of the UFO phenomenon, they suggest. Why, even former President Reagan remarked on several occasions, "I occasionally think how quickly our differences, worldwide, would vanish if we were facing an alien threat from outside this world." First contact could catalyze the formation of a One World government like the one described as being ruled by the Antichrist in End Times prophecy. Besides, is it God or the devil who benefits from these increasing UFO sightings and the subsequent increased belief in extraterrestrial life? Does this lead to an increased belief in God? Or increased unbelief?

You see my point. One thing you learn as a speculative fiction author is that just because a thing is possible or even plausible doesn't mean it will ever actually exist. It still strikes me as improbable, if for no other reason than the fact that it's unnecessary. Occam's Razor and all that. As many speculative novels, including the *Left Behind* series, have demonstrated, Satan could give us a lie we'd all believe with a great deal more subtlety. The extraterrestrial angle is just overkill.

Frankly, Even secular movies have taught us not to trust friendly aliens. The movie *Stargate*, which spawned a whole litter of TV series, gives us the tale of an advanced alien race that gave Earth the leap it needed to build the pyramids. The alien visitors even possessed a technological means of raising humans from the dead. Of course, the catch was that we were slaves to an alien pharaoh. Both versions of the *V* television series showed us alien visitors reminiscent of the contactee movement's Space Brothers who were willing to trade their advanced knowledge for Earth's resources. The catch there was that they were secretly stealing our water and they were in actuality hungry, scaly predators rather than benign benefactors who looked just like us. You see, the problem with alien visitation is that, in reality, they'd probably be here for the food and water... and we're part of the menu.

Even so, *if* the classic Rapture coincides with an extraterrestrial deception (and we naively decide to trust them), this is what I believe *may* occur.

Fallen angels may pose as aliens and will finally "come out" and feed the world a line about how they seeded us and how they've been watching us and will now aid us in the next stage of evolution. I believe they will initiate a purge of religious and philosophical beliefs which contradict them, in the name of evolutionary progress. Those seeds (that religious belief is the evolutionary equivalent of childhood and that atheism is a sort of growing up) have already been planted. Both evolutionists and progressive creationists will be satisfied since both evolution and ID will be given credence (you evolved according to our intelligent design, Earthlings). If the Rapture occurs before or concurrently with their appearance, they may claim the disappearance of Christians is part of the initial purge. They may overcome moral objections to such religious cleansing by invoking the idea that we are in a sense property of theirs since they designed us (lightly accented), but besides that we Christians were some sort of evolutionary throwback or possessed of a mental/evolutionary flaw which was infecting humanity and holding us back from evolutionary Ubermensch (strongly accented).

Of course, there's another scenario that involves an extraterrestrial angle that deserves equal consideration. Let's suppose the classic Rapture occurs. The world unites as we search for answers and as we huddle together against the onslaught of God's Wrath as it is poured out upon the Earth over the next few years. Then one day, as we are immersed in the War to End All Wars, we see the Second Coming. Only someone convinces us that we're seeing an alien invasion. And then they remind everyone that there was a grand abduction event just seven years ago and perhaps they're coming back for the rest of us. Can you imagine the terror of that announcement? In the movie *Skyline* [2010], aliens indiscriminately rapture everyone on Earth with blue hypnotic lights so they can harvest our brains. Yes, you read that right. With scientists such as Stephen Hawking warning us even today that First Contact will be nothing like *Close Encounters of the Third Kind*, and more likely akin to *Independence Day,* we will imagine the worst possible outcome and turn our weapons toward God… which won't last very long, but will certainly fulfill Bible prophecy.

Speculation aside, I personally think the extraterrestrial End Times scenario is a stretch. Again, it's just so unnecessary.

***

Notes

1. Leggett, Paul. "Science Fiction Films: A Cast of Metaphysical Characters," *Christianity Today* 24 (March 21, 1980), p. 32.

2. Doyle, Tom "Christian Apocalyptic Fiction". StrangeHorizons.com (April 8, 2002).Web. Retrieved July 19, 2016.

Tony Breeden

4 Evolution and Science Fiction

When it comes to creationist objections to science fiction, concerns over eschatology and unrealism are just window dressing. At best, they are supporting evidence for their main complaint: Sci-fi is dominated by stories that presume an all-natural history of millions of years of microbes-to-man evolution.

Creationists have objected to sci-fi on the grounds of its evolutionary baggage from the beginning of the modern creation science movement. In one of the earliest references to science fiction by a modern young earth creationist, a two-part article called for *Ex Nihilo* (later named *Creation*) magazine, Graham Leo wrote:

> "Since most science fiction writers are evolutionists or atheists or both, the great majority of science fiction is extremely evolutionary in character.[1]"

> "The majority of Science Fiction is both a rejection of the God who is the Creator/Redeemer, and a desperate quest for a purpose, a meaning, an end, a way out of a seemingly endless and hopeless universe in which belief in impersonal evolution is offered as a basis for and as part of the "only hope" package deal salvation for

mankind.[2]"

The article was called "Evolution and Science Fiction," leaving no doubt in the readers mind that these two concepts should be linked together as enemies of truth. The article was travesty of quote-mining and cherry-picked examples guaranteed to paint science fiction in the worst possible light. At no point were Christian examples of sci-fi offered, nor even examples of sci-fi that deals with Christianity in a positive manner. Heavy-handed articles such as this set the tone for future discussion.

Even today, there is a tendency in conservative Christian circles to blame the public's fascination with little green men on either the implications of Darwinian evolution or the popularity of science fiction itself. Or both.

To be fair, there are glimmers in the darkness. For example, it turns out that Ken Ham is a sci-fi fan (his love of *Doctor Who* has garnered particular attention). Even before that fact came to light, there was a 2007 article by Carl Kerby, called "Science Fiction: Not Just Entertainment.[3]" While the title and byline ("A work of science fiction made me question the existence of a loving God.") both warn of the dangers of science fiction, Kerby's piece was refreshing because it included a reference to CS Lewis' Space Trilogy as an alternative to non-Christian fare and the following admission:

> "God can use fiction—even if it is overtly antibiblical—to bring

about good. Whether they realize it or not, writers who are atheists and evolutionists must borrow biblical concepts in order for their stories to make sense. Even the atheist Isaac Asimov often incorporated Christian elements into his stories... Now that I am a Christian, I look at science fiction through biblical glasses. I can see the evolutionary bias of many science fiction authors. But I can also see Christian themes in many of these same works."

Kerby's point here was followed by a call for discernment, making it one of the few fair-minded articles on the subject. His point reminds me of the fact that God used two pagan kings (Nebuchadnezzar and Cyrus the Great) to fulfill his prophetic will. Likewise, Paul was able to quote the truth contained in the writings of pagan poets on Mars Hill without endorsing everything they wrote.

The other positive reference to science fiction in an *Answers* magazine article by Christian sci-fi author Keith A. Robinson. "The Rise of Apologetics Fiction[4]" notes how Robinson "wanted to honor God by using his imagination to write a science fiction story about what life would be like on a world where evolution had really taken place. That idea became his first novel, Logic's End."

I must say that there are a growing number of

Christian authors who write speculative fiction. Two good places to find some are SpeculativeFaith.com and Robinson's own ApologeticsFiction.com.

Unfortunately, the exceptions do not disprove the general rule: creationist organizations tend present science fiction is a negative light, by either claiming that science fiction is based on evolutionary beliefs or starting points, or by simply using the term as a tongue-in-cheek synonym for evolution itself. In 2005, creation astronomer Jason Lisle did both[5]:

> "Actually, most science fiction is based on the big bang and millions of years of evolution. Indeed, the most famous sci-fi writer of all, H.G. Wells, wrote books on evolution and supported eugenics. In a way, the big bang and evolution are really science fiction, even though they are taught as fact."

Likewise, in an article entitled, "Evolution and the Science of Fiction[6]," Gary Bates, CEO of Creation Ministries International, asked the following:

> "Many wonder (even some Christians)… 'Could there be life on other planets?' But a straightforward reading of Genesis gives us no indication that God created intelligent, alien life-forms elsewhere in the universe. Would

> such questions even be asked if science fiction were not so popular?"

A 1982 study[7] by W.S. Bainbridge found that students who read science fiction are much more likely than other students to believe that contacting extraterrestrial civilizations is both possible and desirable. So there's definitely a correlation between a preference for science fiction and a belief in extraterrestrial life, but is science fiction the cause of the public's fascination with little green men or does it simply fuel our innate curiosity on the subject?

Certainly this appears to be a case of spurious correlation when a preference for science fiction and a belief in extraterrestrial life are both indicators of a segment of the population that has a strong scientific interest overall. In other words, we would expect a segment of the population that has a strong scientific interest to display a preference for science fiction. In today's times, that tendency to believe in the inevitability of extraterrestrial life is reinforced by a modern scientific consensus says the latter is inevitable, but a belief in extraterrestrial life isn't necessarily an indicator of evolutionary belief.

Johannes Kepler was a young earth creationist; thirty years before James Ussher, Kepler wrote *Kanones Pueriles* in which he calculated the universal creation date to be April 27th of 4,997 BC. Most creationists proudly tout his achievements as a scientist (Kepler's Three Laws... not too shabby) and even as an apologist (he dedicated a chapter of his *Mysterium Cosmographicum* to correcting misunderstandings of biblical passages that had been erroneously used as proof texts for geocentrism), but few acknowledge his role as one of the founders of science fiction. Both Isaac Asimov and Carl Sagan have referred to Kepler's *Somnium*, released posthumously by his son in 1636, as the first work of science fiction[8]. *Somnium* details an imagined journey to the moon. While it was written principally to explore how the Earth might look from the Moon, it also included an imaginative exploration of life on the Moon. The Moon is referred to as the island of Levania. Earth is called Volva by the moon's inhabitants. Levanians are sapient creatures with a huge serpentine shape and spongy, porous meat. So, yes, a young earth creationist, writing about the possibility of extraterrestrial alien life, long before Darwin. It would seem that it is neither unnatural nor unreasonable for a man who believes in the Biblical Creator to wonder if that Creator created other races.

Science fiction is a branch of speculative fiction that deals with the future, parallel worlds, new technologies, space travel and extraterrestrials, and often explores the potential consequences of these things. More to the point, as a branch of speculative fiction, science fiction is fiction that asks the eternal question, "What if?"

We've been asking "What if?" questions since long before we ever had a genre of fiction based around it. Ever since man discovered that the moon and the neighboring planets have a surface to walk upon, man has increasingly wondered whether we are alone in the universe and what extraterrestrial life might look like. We wondered about such things long before Charles Darwin came along. Gary Bates has got the cart before the horse! While the current relationship of science and science fiction is more or less reciprocal, there would be no science fiction without scientific speculation. Granted, a lot of sci-fi is more speculation than science, but there's always a springboard of current scientific knowledge from which such speculation proceeds. The more we learn about the world, the more questions we have about it. As our knowledge is refined by later discoveries, we learn to ask better "What if?" questions.

For example, when "canals" on Mars were first described by Italian astronomer Giovanni Schiaparelli in 1877 and then confirmed by later observations, it inspired what I call the Dying Martian Mythos, a body of science fiction that imagined intelligent life on a Mars that was slowly drying out. H.G. Wells' *The War of the Worlds* (1897) doesn't mention the canals but it does describe this slowly dying Mars and their need for earth's resources as being the driving force behind their attempted conquest of Earth. Edgar Rice Burroughs' *A Princess of Mars* (1912), the inspiration for the excellent but critically-maligned Disney film adaptation, *John Carter* (2012), pictures a Mars that is mostly desert with the canals being surrounded by tracts of farmland. C.S. Lewis' *Out of the Silent Planet* (1938), the first book in his Space Trilogy, featured the Martian canals as rifts in a desert world and the only hospitable zones on the planet. Robert Heinlein's *Red Planet* (1949) and Ray Bradbury's *The Martian Chronicles* (1950) both feature the canals as well.

Slowly but surely, the idea of the Martian canals began to lose favor, until finally the United States' *Mariner 4* took pictures of the surface of Mars in 1965 which absolutely dispelled the notion of their being anything but optical illusions. Nowadays, Martian canals aren't even featured in science fiction because the springboard of fact prevents it. Science fiction didn't continue to proliferate the idea of Martian canals because science fiction deals with future possibilities, not obsolete fantasies.

Based on this premise, some evolutionists have objected to creationism in science fiction at all. For example, on the Ecology & Evolution blog written by members of the School of Natural Sciences, Trinity College (Dublin, Ireland), Jesko Zimmerman wrote an article entitled, "Creationism in Science Fiction: Artistic freedom or anti-science?[9]"

In this article, Zimmerman wrote the following:

> "I think that the most important element in science fiction is exploration: take the now, look at our social, scientific and technological achievements and make a step forward. …The defining element is that it is a fictional continuation of our

> current knowledge, exploring whatever implications the creator of the work wants to explore.
>
> And there lies my problem with Creationism."

Zimmerman's believes that the danger of including creationism or even Intelligent Design in science fiction is that it "gives those fans who do not have a scientific background a false impression of realism associated with creationism, spreading anti-science further." One notes that this is almost identical to the reason given for why evolutionists should not debate creationists. It smacks of having a glass chin. If I believed I had the better argument, I wouldn't care who thought the other position was valid or not at the outset; the point of the debate would be to sway them to my side!

Despite all of the rhetoric about creationism being anti-science, it remains an historical fact that founders of modern science – people like Bacon, Newton, Pascal, Lord Kelvin, Maxwell, Linnaeus, Faraday, and Boyle – were Creationists who wanted to, as Johann Kepler himself put it, "think God's thoughts after Him."

In any case, Zimmerman's charge of creationism as anti-science, common as it is, is based on the idea that Darwin's theory has usurped creationism and that we ought to move on. The trouble is that millions of years of microbes-to-man evolution is based on the premise of pure naturalism. Critics of creationism and ID fail to realize that science chained to naturalism can only give us all-natural answers that may or may not be true – and are certainly false where the supernatural was involved! The trouble is that the assumption of pure naturalism is blind; that is, it cannot tell us when the supernatural should be called for instead of the natural answer because it cannot ever consider the supernatural as a valid answer. It puts one in mind of Laurence J. Peter's remark that "maybe an atheist cannot find God for the same reason a thief cannot find a policeman[10]."

Incidentally, naturalism is contradictory: its adherents must affirm that naturalism can do supernatural things no one's ever observed; like everything coming from nothing (or from comic book multiverses), life coming from non-life, or that an amphibian may at long last become a human being of noble birth! By contrast, even Thomas H. Huxley, known as Darwin's Bulldog, and certainly no friend of religion, conceded that special creation was quite reasonable, given the existence of a Deity[11]. We also must not forget that a Creator is an artist. Just as Da Vinci didn't have to paint the Mona Lisa as a baby and then wait for her to grow up on canvas, God is perfectly able to create the cosmos with the level of maturity He so desired.

It might interest you to know that both of the examples of creationism in sci-fi that Zimmerman identified (Ridley Scott's 2012 *Prometheus* movie and the 2004 *Battlestar Galactica* TV series reboot, respectively) are considered secular rather than Christian fare. I've read a lot of critical reviews of both from Christian apologists and media critics complaining about how these secular offerings get the creationism wrong, but I've yet to see quality sci-fi film offerings from Christians that we might refer folks to instead.

Most folks don't realize that comic book heroes are science fiction. Predominantly, such fiction at this point explains super beings with evolutionary appeals to the "next stage of human development." Oddly, these folks seem to have a single gene that is, typically, triggered by the onset of puberty, or by a dose of radiation that somehow doesn't result in cancer, birth defects, sterility or agonizing death, AND somehow gives us abilities as varied as bending spoons with our minds, sprouting wings or turning invisible… which is not really how microbes-to-man evolution is supposed to work. For that matter, when we're told that these mutations are an example of fish-to-philosopher evolution, we should keep in mind that a single mutation, no matter how cool it is (and real mutations are usually either harmful or benign) isn't really evolution. By the way, don't you love how scientists in fictional settings always conveniently know they're looking at the "next stage in evolution"?

Still, there are lots of phenomenon and alleged human abilities that defy conventional explanation. How would we explain this in a Biblical context? Oh, demonic possession is a tempting answer. And I think it's been done. It brings to mind the Biblical passage where Moses' rod turned into a snake and the pharaoh's magicians duplicated the feat. But if not divine or demonic intervention, how would we explain such phenomenon such as telepathy or levitation, if it ever developed? Would we capitulate to Darwin, or do we have a viable alternative theory? Is this potential locked away in all mankind, prohibited lest our sin nature allow us to use this power for great harm? I think it's worth exploring, which is precisely why I wrote *Johnny Came Home*! In doing so, I also explored the moral implications of Darwin's theory, commented on races from a Biblical perspective and noted what it means to be human. All because I set out to tell an entertaining story from a Christian mythos.

All because I didn't toss out the baby with the bathwater.

In the minds of many Christians, the very idea of alien life is synonymous with an evolutionary worldview; but ought this to be the case? It is true that the idea of extraterrestrial life is consistent with an evolutionary worldview. That does not mean it's necessarily inconsistent with a Biblical worldview. A Creator such as the Bible describes might conceivably have more than one canvass! Would the existence of alien life prove microbe-to-man evolution is true? Would it invalidate the Bible with irreconcilable theological problems? Some folks certainly think so, but I think this is a false dichotomy, as I shall attempt to demonstrate in the rest of this book.

***

Notes

1. Graham, Leo. "Evolution and Science Fiction – Part 1." *Creation* Vol. 5, No. 3 (January 1983), pp. 16-18.

2. Graham, Leo. "Evolution and Science Fiction – Part 2: The Role of God." *Creation* Vol. 5, no 4 (April 1983): 22-25.

3. Kerby, Carl. "Science Fiction – Not Just Entertainment." AnswersinGenesis.org. December 6, 2007. Web. Retrieved July 19, 2016.

4. Robinson, Keith A. "The Rise of Apologetics Fiction." *Answers* magazine. Vol 7. No. 2 (July-September 2012), p. 1

5. Lisle, Jason. "Science Fact? Or Science Fiction?" *AnswersinGenesis.org.* February 25, 2005, Web. Retrieved July 19, 2016.

6. Bates, Gary. "Evolution and the science of fiction: A denial of the awesome Creator." Creation 25(1):54–55 December 2002. As cited from Creation.com/evolution-and-the-science-of-fiction. Accessed 24 Feb 2016.

7. Bainbridge, William Sims (1982). "The Impact of Science Fiction on Attitudes

Toward Technology". In Emme, Eugene Morlock. *Science fiction and space futures: past and present.* Univelt. The same study found a strong correlation between a preference for science fiction and support for the space program.

8. By comparison, Mary Wollstonecraft Shelley's *Frankenstein*, popularly held as the first work of science fiction, wasn't written until 1818, almost two centuries later.

9. Zimmerman, Jesko. "Creationism in Science Fiction: Artistic freedom or anti-science?" EcoEvo@TDC. 19 Sep 2014. Web: http://www.ecoevoblog.com/2014/09/19/creationism-in-science-fiction-artistic-freedom-or-anti-science/. Retrieved 29 Feb 2016.

10. Peter, Laurence J. Peter's Quotations: Ideas for Our Times. Harper Collins. (1993), p. 44. Commenting on a quote by Francis Thompson: "An atheist is a man who believes himself an accident."

11. Huxley, Thomas H. Quoted in Leonard. Huxley, *Life and Letters of Thomas Henry Huxley*, Vol. II (1903), p. 241.

Part 2: Why UFOs Are Not the Issue

5 Chasing the Flying Saucers

Some folks claim that we're arguing a non-issue. They believe that the fact of extraterrestrial life has been established by the number of UFO reports given over the years.

A total of 12, 618 sightings were reported to The US Air Force's Project Blue Book[1], headquartered at Wright-Patterson Air Force Base, from 1947 until the project was shut down in 1969. After the reports were investigated, only 701 of these sightings remain truly "Unidentified." That's about five percent.

Now, that doesn't automatically mean that these UFOs are visitors from another world. There is a vast difference between a flying saucer and a UFO, the latter of which is merely an Unidentified Flying Object, an aerial event for which we lack sufficient evidence to conclusively identify. To conflate UFOs with flying saucers (or any other extraterrestrial vehicles) would be a logical leap of, well, astronomical proportions!

For a time, West Virginia Ufologist Gray Barker wrote a column called "Chasing the Flying Saucers" for Ray Palmer's *Flying Saucers* magazine. The banner featured a cartoon illustration of Barker running after a flying saucer with a butterfly net. Meanwhile a little green man with a butterfly net of his own was leaning down out of a saucer behind Barker! I don't think any other illustration quite captures the sorry state of a person who attempts to unravel the riddle of the saucers. Except perhaps Alice and her rabbit hole.

In the very first issue of his own UFO magazine, *The Saucerian* (September 1953), Barker noted that "Saucertruth is so much stranger than fiction, most people think it is fiction." There are crackpot conspiracy theories and genuine cover-ups, mistakes, hallucinations and hoaxes, rabbit trails and genuine mysteries enough to keep the most ardent saucerian chasing in circles. At times it seems like an unanswerable mystery; at other times, you're convinced that you've stumbled upon the secret… or that it's all a fraud.

I make no bones about the fact that where saucers are concerned, I am cheerfully skeptical. I don't think UFOs have anything to do with little green (or grey) men from another world, but I'd be happy to be proven wrong! I think we need to take Barker's (original[2]) approach to the subject. He ended his first *Saucerian* editorial with these words:

> "For while our eyes may reach for
> the stars, we faithfully promise to
> keep our feet firmly implanted
> upon the ground."

I think most of us err on the side of being too grounded or having our head too close to the stars. It's helpful to take a step back and take a look at the possibilities.

There are several ways we might account for truly unidentified UFOs:

1. A good number are likely misidentified objects of a much more mundane nature. By this, we mean everyday things that are already commonly experienced, like clouds, weather balloons, comets, commercial or known military aircraft, et cetera. Atmospheric phenomena are often mistaken for flying saucers, particularly lenticular clouds, ball lightning, St. Elmo's Fire, and Fata Morgana mirages, a rare phenomenon in which images of objects such as mountains, cities and ships are refracted from beyond the horizon.

There is the possibility that some UFOs are secret government projects. These would be real government aircraft like the stealth bomber, Skyhook weather balloons, et cetera, which have been retroactively confirmed to have accounted for many previously unidentified aerial objects once they were declassified. Mundane objects and phenomena account for an estimated 90 to 95 percent of UFO sightings. Essentially UFOs become IFOs (Identified

Flying Objects). Any Ufologist who insists that ALL or even most UFO sightings are the real McCoy is an unrealistic true believer.

The principle of mediocrity could be applied here; since an overwhelming majority of UFOs end up having mundane explanations, the most likely explanation for the remainder of unexplained sightings would also be mundane in nature.

2. There are also psychological considerations. In other words, some could be hallucinations. Likewise, cultural expectations can influence what we think we see. For example, prior to the release of Steven Spielberg's *Close Encounters of the Third Kind* (1977), there were no records of Greys with long, thin necks in UFO literature[3], but they started popping up after the movie featured them in the final scenes.

Another psychological consideration is that many contactee and abductee accounts apparently occur while the subject is in a trance. Some contactee cases evidence clues that the subject is suffering from schizophrenia or epilepsy. Tellingly, the technology described in such experiences usually contemporaneous with the subject's idea of high tech; thus, earlier contactees described magnetic tape and knobs for cockpit controls, while newer accounts include more modern ideas of advanced technology. Unless the aliens are advancing at the same technological rate we are (you know, despite their ability to traverse the stars), this either suggests that they are either hiding their true technology behind a façade of whatever we think of as advanced tech at the time or, more likely, the notions of alien tech are derived from the person's subconscious during an aforementioned trance. If the setting isn't real, how can we be sure the experience was a genuine memory?

3. A minor theory regarding objects in the sky is that they are actually elusive biological entities that are either terrestrial, extraterrestrial or extradimensional in origin. The terrestrial origins theory would imply that they are cryptids. It seems doubtful that we have missed the classification of aerial entities of this nature; however, proponents of this theory suggest that these organism defy traditional biological classification. In any case, this theory would only account for objects in the sky and not the contactee/abductee aspect of Ufology.

4. With apologies to Marty McFly, I should mention that time traveler theory. Yes, there are folks who suppose that the UFO phenomenon is the product of time travelers from the future, sent back in time to do, well, Heaven knows what. It's been proposed that they're correcting the genome through abductions, coming to warn us of a future cataclysm, or even that they're simply bored and want to tour a bit of the past. A lot of the time traveler theory is a leftover from the days of the benevolent "Space Brothers." West Virginia native Woodrow Derenberger claimed that he had been in contact with a time travelling alien named Indrid Cold from the planet Lanulos, which turned out to be, as John

Keel put it, "a pleasant little planet where the people ran around nearly nude[4]." Derenberger's extraterrestrials were actually alleged to be orphaned Earthmen from our future. As Derenberger wrote in the November 1968 issue of *Probe*[5]:

"They believe their forefathers came from Earth in a space ship and after they had landed, somehow lost the art of space travel. It was many, many years before they again learned how to travel in space."

So they were from the future where we have the technology to build a spaceship, got marooned in the "Ganymede galaxy" (which doesn't exist, of course, Ganymede being one of Jupiter's moons), lost and regained that technology, and were now visiting Earth again. To make matters worse, apparently time on Lanulos works differently from Earth time, so that Cold and his associates had to make their visits brief if they didn't want to grow too young to recall how to operate their spacecraft!

On a more serious note, some folks have actually suggested that, despite contactee accounts like Derenberger's hoax[6], that time travel best explains the fact that UFO visits are apparent frequent but brief. Others have suggested an added time travel element to proposed extraterrestrial visits, compounding the problem of proof but distancing the UFO phenomenon from falsification. In other words, it could be true, but who could ever prove or disprove such fantastic speculation?

5. Purely supernatural non-demonic causes have been proposed for UFOs, but the Biblical position on

the afterlife seems prohibitive to the very possibility of ghosts. Specifically, Paul states that to be absent from the body is to be present with the Lord [2 Corinthians 5:8] and Christ spoke from the cross to the repentant thief, "Today, you will be with me in Paradise."

Ghosts as restless human souls are prohibited by Biblical text. While the disciples thought they were seeing a ghost at first when they saw Jesus walking on water, it was Jesus after all and not a spirit. And while King Saul thought he was talking to the ghost of the prophet Samuel through the Witch of Endor, it was an evil spirit and not Samuel at all. It must be said that in cases where the supernatural entities are beings from another plane of existence, such as the Etherians of UFO cult literature, such beings are, from a Christian perspective, indistinguishable from demons.

A possibility that would not contradict Scripture could be that ghosts are temporal echoes, rather like the after image on television screen. A lot of ghost stories involve ghosts that simply repeat a pattern each night, going down the same path, appearing in the same window. In the case of these hauntings, maybe an echo of sorts is preserved. In this respect, the ghost would be something like a picture or recording of a person, but really not the person itself except in a superficial appearance as such.

6. In some cases, particularly those where no contactees or abductees are involved, we could be seeing some of the "wonders in the heavens" [Acts

2:19-20] promised in the Bible as a sign of the End of Days. If this is the case, then we are projecting a bit when we see these lights and presume they are manned. In the book of Exodus, the Hebrew children were preceded through the desert by a pillar of cloud by day and a pillar of fire by night, a sign of God's presence with them. The Bible also promises that in the latter days, there will be signs in the heavens, things like the darkening of the sun, the moon turning the color of blood, and something that sounds very much like a meteorite striking the earth. It's not outside the realm of possibility that UFO lights could be part of such heavenly wonders and that their true purpose is to harbinger the End of Days.

7. We may be looking at interdimensional beings (i.e., entities from beyond the dimensions of space-time). A lot of UFO researchers are abandoning the extraterrestrial hypothesis in favor of an extra-dimensional hypothesis. The extra-dimensional hypothesis would explain how UFOs can vanish and appear so suddenly and why they seem to defy the laws of physics. One candidate for these alleged interdimensional beings are angels. Many Christians will object that angels inhabit the supernatural realm not a dimension of this universe, but that could be semantics based on a pre-scientific understanding of such things. Given the traumatic nature of abduction stories, the anti-Christian message of the "aliens," and the fact that so-called abductions can be stopped at the mention of the name of Jesus Christ[7], the extra-dimensional hypothesis may be a synonym for

a Satanic deception conducted by fallen angels. This is the most widely accepted theory for truly unexplained UFOs within conservative Christianity.

8. We may be looking at actual extraterrestrial aircraft and/or phenomena. You know, textbook UFOs piloted by Extraterrestrial Biological Entities (EBEs).

This seems entirely unlikely to me. I'm not alone. In his book, *The Demon-Haunted World*, Carl Sagan characterized the notion that "alien beings from distant worlds visit the Earth with casual impunity" as pseudoscience[8]. In support of his convictions, he cited a 1969 review of the University of Colorado's 1968 *Report on Unidentified Flying Objects* (more commonly known as the *Condon Report*) by the National Academy of Sciences, which concurred with the former's conclusion that "On the basis of present knowledge the least likely explanation of UFOs is the hypothesis of extraterrestrial visitations by intelligent beings.[9]"

For the sake of record, the conclusions of Project Blue Book are that[10]:

> (1) no UFO reported, investigated, and evaluated by the Air Force has ever given any indication of threat to our national security;
>
> (2) there has been no evidence submitted to or discovered by the Air Force that sightings categorized as "unidentified"

represent technological developments or principles beyond the range of present-day scientific knowledge; and

(3) there has been no evidence indicating that sightings categorized as "unidentified" are extraterrestrial vehicles.

9. Last but not least, some of those as-yet-unidentified flying objects could be hoaxes and frauds. As skeptic Michael Shermer noted, "Sometimes people just make stuff up.[11]" Such hoaxes can carry on for decades without being exposed.

West Virginia has its share of storytellers. Even church-going mountain folk are not above pulling a fellow's leg. In fact, every year at the Vandalia Gathering, a Liar's Contest is held that generally draws standing room only crowds. The fellow with the best story gets a Golden Shovel.

As we will see, there are quite a few folks in Ufological circles who deserve an honorary Golden Shovel. Chief among the potential candidates for a Lifetime Achievement Award is West Virginia native Gray Barker[12], author of *They Knew Too Much About Flying Saucers* (1956). Barker was infamous for various UFO frauds and hoaxes, several of which were not uncovered until after his death in 1984. These included the infamous letter from "R.E. Straith" delivered to George Adamski on official government letterhead from the Cultural Exchange Committee" (which does not exist), which erroneously confirmed Adamski's contactee claims and encouraged him to keep up his work.

Certainly, George Adamski's tale of a fair-haired Venusian named Orthon took many folks "hook, line and saucer" in the 1950s. His first two UFO books, *Flying Saucers have Landed* (1953, with Desmond Leslie) and *Inside the Space Ships* (1955) were bestsellers. In October 1957, Barker's good friend Jim Moseley printed a Special Adamski Expose issue of *Saucer News* that provided evidence that the whole thing was a fraud. The issue included testimony from Adamski's associates that his famous photographs of flying saucers were falsified and then went one step further, showing how an Adamski saucer photo could be produced using a model made from a Chrysler hubcap, a coffee can, and ping pong balls.

Adamski supporters remained unconvinced. When the Straith Letter appeared, they touted it as proof that the charges against Adamski were unfounded. Never mind that *Inside the Space Ships* is basically a "non-fiction" remake of a science fiction book Adamski had published back in 1949 called *Pioneers in Space*.

In his 1967 *Book of Adamski,* Gray Barker referred to the Straith Letter as "one of the great unsolved mysteries of the UFO field[13]." He knew better, of course. Co-conspirator Jim Moseley warned Barker that he would confess the whole thing in the event that Barker died, which he dutifully performed in the January 10, 1985 issue of *Saucer Smear*. Apparently, in December 1957, seven fake letters were drafted to various persons in the UFO community and Jim Moseley's father. Only six were sent. Moseley wisely forgot to mail the one addressed to his father[14].

When Barker wrote more about the Straith Letter in the *Book of Adamski*, claiming that "Due to my unpleasant experiences with it and the distrust I suffered as a result of it, I wanted to forget about it and have kept these facts to myself for nine long years. If somebody or some agency was after ME, they have failed for I have survived.[15]" His complaint regarding distrust seems to be a half-hidden reference to the fact that Lonzo Dove linked the Straith Letter to Barker's typewriter as earlier as June 1959 in a *Saucer News* article that also accused Barker of having hoaxed the original Men in Black incident involving Albert K. Bender. Unfortunately, Dove was only able to make the accusation against Barker. His promised follow-up article proving the case was squelched by Barker's co-conspirator, Jim Moseley, who refused to print the story in *Saucer News*[16]. As for unpleasant experiences involving an agency that was after Barker, it wasn't the Men in Black, as he implied. Rather the FBI investigated both Barker and Moseley, mostly because unauthorized use of official government stationary is a crime. Barker smashed the incriminating typewriter and deposited the pieces in a construction site somewhere in Clarksburg, WV[17]. The FBI eventually dropped the case due to lack of evidence.

Barker and Mosely also hoaxed a film of a flying saucer, allegedly taken on July 3, 1966 near Lost Creek, WV. In reality, the bogus saucer was attached to a fishing pole held by John Sheets, one of Barker's researchers, while Moseley drove the car and Barker filmed. Moseley notes that the Lost Creek film got a lot of attention.

> "In addition to showing the film on New York–area television and at one of the Saucer News monthly lectures, I incorporated it and the story behind it into my American Program Bureau talk."

Barker also used it as a visual in his lectures and sold prints of the film. The film continued to be used until about 1975, when Moseley stopped lecturing[18]. That particular hoax wasn't exposed until 1995, when Ralph Coon's documentary film on Gray Barker, *Whispers From Space*, let the cat out of the bag.

Perhaps encouraged by Moseley's revelation of the Straith Letter hoax, John C. Sherwood confessed[19] to his part in another. Apparently, he sent Gray a sci-fi story in 1968, dealing with UFOs as time machines. Barker convinced Sherwood to "make the incident seem real by creating a fictitious organization out of whole cloth," to nix the confession at the end that revealed the entire story was made up, and to "make it as technical as possible to make it look like a real scientific report." Sherwood dutifully did as he was urged, writing as the fake scientist Dr. Richard H. Pratt and even going so far as to announce the formation of Pratt's flying saucer club, B.I.C.R., in a letter to Raymond E. Palmer's *Flying Saucer* magazine. "Flying Saucers: Time Machines," by "Dr. Richard H. Pratt," was published in the Spring/Summer 1969 issue of Barker's magazine *Saucer News* (which he had since purchased from Moseley), followed by "The Strange B.I.C.R. Affair" in the Summer 1970 issue. Writing about Richard H. Pratt in his final book, *Men in Black: The Secret Terror Among Us* (1983), Barker shamelessly mentions John Sherwood as "a young investigator and UFO author" who lived in the same Michigan town that B.I.C.R. listed as its address. In a footnote, Gray also wrote, "Although I have exchanged three letters with [John Sherwood] during the past two years, he has never answered or commented upon my queries concerning Pratt's article[20]." As if to bait Sherwood further, Barker wrote that "I have never discounted the possibility that the whole Pratt business was an elaborate leg-pull perpetrated on me and my readers, though I can't imagine why somebody would have gone to that much trouble" and goes on to suggest that B.I.C.R. "evidently was real, since the group advertised in *Flying Saucers*.[21]"

Even so, it wouldn't be until 1998, roughly fourteen years after Barker's death and nearly thirty years after the fraud was first accomplished, that Sherwood would cop to the his part in the hoax.

It goes without saying that Barker isn't the only person ever to perpetrate a UFO hoax. For example, 1991 two fellows named Doug Bower and David Chorley[22] admitted to creating crop circles throughout England, trampling down the wheat using only "two wooden boards, a piece of string and a bizarre sighting device attached to a baseball cap." Prior to their confession, one of their circles was publicly authenticated by a UFO investigator as having been made by a "superior intelligence." I'm sure Bower and Chorley appreciated the compliment! Since then, there have been copycats across the globe, but true believers suppose that humans account for only part of the phenomenon. Even this small list of hoaxes suffices to show that a really good hoax can go on for decades – if the truth of it is ever uncovered at all!

So there we have it:

1. Misidentified terrestrial, technological and meteorological subjects
2. Psychological effects
3. Cryptids
4. Time travelers
5. Supernatural activity (i.e., ghosts)
6. Biblically foretold "wonders in the heavens"
7. Interdimensional beings (such as angels, fallen or otherwise)

8. Actual extraterrestrial craft (however unlikely.)
9. Hoaxes

For the record, I do not think there is a magic bullet for the UFO phenomenon; that is, it is unlikely that there is a one-size-fits-all solution for all truly unexplained UFO accounts. Painting the UFO enigma with a single wide brush only evidences one's desire to have a pat answer!

Having said that, like it or not, there has been no solid scientific evidence to support what is called the Extraterrestrial Hypothesis (ETH), that aliens are visiting this planet and have done so for a long, long time. Almost all cases of alleged extraterrestrial phenomena end up having a more mundane cause. As to the remainder, a bit of special pleading is simply tacked on when there is insufficient evidence for a more mundane cause, even if there is no definitive evidence of extraterrestrials either! One can almost hear the *History Channel*'s crazy-haired Giorgio A. Tsoukalos proclaiming "It must be aliens!"

My fellow Christians will likely agree with my assessment of ETH, but in all fairness we have to ask: Is Tsoukalos' mantra any less reductionist than the claim that "the UFO phenomenon is 100% demonic[23]"?

The next few chapters seek to answer that very question.

***

Notes

1. "Unidentified Flying Objects – Project Blue Book." National Archives. http://www.archives.gov/research/military/air-force/ufos.html#usafac. Accessed 24 Feb 2016.

2. Gray Barker later became a notorious hoaxer but he began as a serious UFO investigator.

3. Kottmeyer, Martin S. "Pencil-Neck Aliens." REALL.org. February 1993. http://www.reall.org/newsletter/v01/n01/pencil-neck-aliens.html. Retrieved September 15, 2016.

4. Keel, John A. *The Mothman Prophecies*. Tor edition (2001), p. 113.

5. Derenberger, Woodrow W. "I Met a Man From Another World!" *Probe* 5, 1 (September 1968), pp. 8-11.

6. See Chapter 8.

7. The CE4 Research Group, through research conducted with over 350 abductees, found that "The experience was shown to be able to be stopped or terminated by calling on the name and authority of JESUS CHRIST. Not as a magic word but by their allegiance to and personal relationship with Him." Quoted from "Close Encounters of the Fourth Kind - Alien Abduction: The Unwanted Piece of the

UFO Puzzle." *AlienResistance.org*. Web. Retrieved July 20, 2016.

8. Sagan, Carl. *The Demon Haunted World: Science as a Candle in the Dark*. Ballantine Books. Reprint Edition (1997), p. 43.

9. *Ibid.*, p. 93.

10. See Note 1.

11. McRobbie, Linda Rodriguez. "Why Alien Abductions Are Down Dramatically." *Boston Globe* (June 12, 2016). Web. Retrieved July 26, 2016. Michael Shermer repeated the quote in a tweet dated June 23, 2016, clarifying the quote with the note, "(e.g., science fiction)." https://twitter.com/michaelshermer/status/746057576958279680.

12. Gray Barker is a fascinating trickster. My forthcoming book, *The Truth is Fantastic!*, relates how much of UFO and science fiction culture can be traced back to this fellow West Virginian.

13. Barker, Gray. *The Book of Adamski*. Saucerian Publications (1967), p. 77.

14. Moseley, James, and Karl T Pflock. Shockingly Close to the Truth: Confessions of a Grave-Robbing Ufologist. (2002), pp. 124-25.

15. Barker (1967), *Ibid.*

16. Moseley (2002), pp.126-127.

17. *Ibid.*, p.126.

18. *Ibid*, pp.199-201.

19. Sherwood, John C. "Gray Barker: My Friend, the Myth-Maker." *Skeptical Inquirer.* Vol 22.3 (May/June 1988). Web. Retrieved March 16, 2016.

20. Barker, Gray. *Men in Black: The Secret terror Among Us.* Saucerian Books (1983). Reprinted by Metadisc Books (2011), p. 125

21. *Ibid.*, p. 132.

22. Schmidt, William E. "2 'Jovial Con Men' Demystify Those Crop Circles in Britain." *New York Times.* 10 September 1991.

23. Scott, Jefferson. "UFOs and the Christian Worldview." *JeffersonScott.com.* Web. Retrieved July 21, 2016.

Tony Breeden

6 Look To the Skies!

In most people's minds, the UFO phenomena as we know it began on June 24, 1947, when Kenneth Arnold spotted strange, crescent-shaped aerial objects near Mt. Rainier, Washington. He described their motion as "erratic, like a saucer if you skip it across the water." The media quickly muddled this description even as it sensationalized the sighting, until the "flying saucer" was born. Generally, a journalist named Bill Bequette is blamed for origin of the mix-up, though the term "flying saucer" itself never appeared in his early news story.

Afterward, the US experienced its first official UFO flap (a term for a high frequency of saucer sightings in a relatively small period of time). Among the news stories at the time were the Roswell saucer crash and the Maury Island affair, the latter of which was also connected to Kenneth Arnold.

Kenneth Arnold, Roswell & Maury Island

On June 21, 1947, three days before Arnold's sighting, Fred Crisman and Harold Dahl reported falling debris and threats by men in black following sightings of "donut-shaped" UFOs over Maury Island in Puget Sound. After receiving samples of the debris from Crisman, *Fate* magazine editor Raymond E. Palmer contacted Arnold to investigate. Some have suggested that Palmer's involvement in the Maury Island affair was suspicious. After all, he'd crossed paths with one of the two witnesses prior to the investigation. While Palmer was editor at

Amazing Stories, Fred Crisman wrote to the magazine with a tale of how he battled a subterranean race of creatures called the dero during World War II in order to escape a cave in Burma. Also, it is suspected that Palmer was responsible for the news stories that broke about the incident on July 8, 1947 as they read much like a press release. And again, the samples that supposedly came from the saucer were sent directly to Palmer, who was secretly trying to launch *Fate* magazine while he was still the editor at *Amazing Stories* and needed a big story. Arnold's story was big, but it was yesterday's news. He intended to piggyback this new saucer story off Arnold's fame. Alas! The initial release of the Maury Island UFO had the bad luck of being fed to the newswires on the same day as the alleged Roswell, New Mexico saucer crash and was eclipsed by the more sensational news.

Roswell wasn't as big a deal as it is presented today. Yes, the press initially gave it headlines like "RAAF Captures Flying Saucer On Ranch in Roswell Region" (*Roswell Daily Record*), but the press release was inaccurate. For starters, it claimed that a disc had landed. There was no disc, but rather a "large area of bright wreckage made up of rubber strips, tinfoil, a rather tough paper and sticks." And in case you missed that bit about the "wreckage," it was a crash, not a landing. The story died the next day, when the Army explained that the wreckage had been identified as a weather balloon.

As it turns out, it was a bit more than a weather

balloon. In 1995, it was found that the debris at Roswell was consistent with a balloon from Project Mogul. Mogul's purpose was the long-distance detection of sound waves generated by Soviet atomic bomb tests. It was understandably top secret and definitely not something the government wanted to the public (or especially the Soviets) to know about; hence the cover-up.

Nick Redfern has written a book called *Body Snatchers in the Desert: The Horrible Truth at the Heart of the Roswell Story* (2005), which I find disturbingly plausible. Most conspiracy buffs and Ufologists are familiar with the fact that at the end of World War II, the US government snatched up German scientists like Dr. Wernher Von Braun in Operation Paperclip. On the one hand, Paperclip and similar initiatives allowed the US to keep advanced military technology out of Soviet hands and paved the way for the space race. This technology included Nazi flying saucer prototypes like the *Haunebu* saucer and the crescent-shaped *Parabola* craft built by German brothers Walter and Reimar Horten. On the other hand, Paperclip allowed Nazi scientists on US soil. Understandably, the US government didn't let the public know about this deal with the Devil for several decades.

According to Redfern's research, we did something similar to Paperclip with the Japanese. In particular, he points out that Japan had been working on the Fugo balloon project. Japan launched 9000 high altitude balloons armed with explosive devices, about a hundred of which touched down on US soil. There were few casualties and the Fugo balloons were kept out of the media to prevent a panic. There were plans were Fugo balloons armed with bioweapons.

The probable source of these bioweapons was Japan's infamous Unit 731. Sanctioned human experimentation conducted by Unit 731 involved live vivisection, experiments to determine the effects of frostbite, high altitude pressurization, exposure to bioweapons, flamethrowers, and explosives. Some of these experiments were conducted on U.S. POWs. Others were conducted on persons with disabilities.

Redfern connects these dots to the NEPA (Nuclear Energy for Propulsion Aircraft) program. Basically, the US built prototypes for and conducted experiments related to the piloting nuclear powered aircraft. Prisoners and mental patients from U.S jails and institutions were used for the human trials, along with dead bodies snatched from morgues and hospitals without consent of surviving kin. This body snatching program was dubbed Project Sunshine. Redfern provided documentary evidence that some of the "specimens" came from Formosa, home of Unit 731.

With this background information in mind, he believes that the Roswell crash was a cover-up for a prototype hybrid craft. Basically, it was a balloon array carrying a light-bodied aircraft, possibly adapted from the Horten Parabola designs. He believes that it crashed in the desert and that the bodies found were persons with progeria. Werner syndrome or "adult progeria" is more common in Japan. Those with progeria tend to be hairless, have large heads and small bodies. Redfern suggests that the large-headed, small-bodied "aliens" with Oriental features were in fact persons with disabilities used for human flight experiments, likely "recruited" through the ungodly body-snatching program called Project Sunshine. NEPA was a failure, by the way.

Redfern suggested that the UFO angle was pushed to cover the fact that we were conducting human experiments with the help of Japanese war criminals and Nazis on our payroll. He further suggests that the Majestic documents and other false UFO evidence was planted by the government in an elaborate attempt trying to throw the Soviets off the scent.

But again, Roswell was a blip on the radar back then. Meanwhile, Arnold began his investigation of the Maury Island incident.

The basics of the story were that on June 21, 1947, Harold Dahl, his teenage son, two crewman and the family dog were patrolling the harbor in Puget Sound. At about 2:00 PM that day, Dahl spotted six doughnut shaped objects with portholes or windows around the edges hovering in the air over Maury Island. As they watched, five of the UFOs began circling the sixth, which appeared to be having mechanical problems, after which pieces of metallic debris began falling out of the afflicted vessel. The debris killed Dahl's dog, burned his son's arm and damaged the boat. Dahl managed to collect some of the debris and to take photographs of the UFOs, the latter of which ended up being marred with white spots "as if exposed to radiation."

Fred Lee Crisman was not happy about his boat and did not initially believe the story, until Dahl gave him the evidence. Crisman claimed that he went to the beach the next day and found more of the debris – and also saw a saucer! Crisman offered to sell the saucer debris to Ray Palmer, who, again, hired THE Kenneth Arnold to investigate. Arnold arrived on July 29, 1947. Arnold called upon Captain E.J. Smith to help him with the investigation, who arrived on July 31, 1947.

Dahl was originally reluctant to speak to them. He claimed that about 4 or 5 days after the sighting he'd been contacted by a man in a black suit who drove a new 1947 Buick. Dahl had the impression that he was a representative of the military or government. Dahl claimed the man told him details of the UFO sighting that had not yet been made public and warned him to forget all about everything he had seen on or near Maury Island. This was the first alleged case of the "Men in Black," also known as the Silence group.

Despite the Man in Black's threat, Dahl and Crisman shared his story with Arnold and Smith. Notably and strangely, they lied about being harbor patrolmen during the interview. Unsure whether it was a hoax, Arnold brought in Air Force intelligence officer,

Lieutenant Frank Brown and Captain William Davidson, who had interviewed Arnold after his own sighting. The officers recognized the debris as ordinary aluminum but didn't wish to embarrass Arnold. Arnold himself recounted later that they weren't a bit interested in the debris and left the hotel without any samples. If Crisman hadn't shown up with a Kellogg's corn flakes box [yes, you read that correctly] full of debris fragments, they wouldn't have taken anything with them at all.

The Maury Island affair made headlines again when on August 1, 1947 the plane carrying the intelligence officers and the corn flakes box of evidence crashed, killing Brown and Davidson. They were the first casualties of the newly formed U.S. Air Force military branch. The Air Force and the FBI began an intense investigation of the crash and the Maury Island UFO claims

Meanwhile *Tacoma Times* reporter Paul Lantz began receiving calls, beginning an hour after the crash, from someone who told him the names of the officers killed in the crash before the Air Force released their names. The anonymous caller also said the plane was shot down by a 20 mm cannon and connected it to the Maury Island affair. The following day, the *Times* ran a story by Lantz entitled, "Sabotage Hinted in Crash of Army Bomber at Kelso" The sub-headline read, "Plane May Hold Flying Disk Secret."

Jerome Clark[1] reports that when Associated Press reporter Elmer Vogel questioned Dahl on the subject, Dahl's wife brandished a butcher knife and told her husband, "I'm tired of being embarrassed by your lies! Tell this man the truth." Dahl then admitted he'd lied. An FBI report date August 19, 1947, relates essentially the same tale and further notes that Vogel "advised the Boise Statesman shortly before, or at the time Kenneth Arnold left Boise to come to Tacoma to check on the flying disc stories with Dahl and Crisman, that Arnold should not come as the entire story was a hoax."

The Air Force investigation also found the Maury Island account to be a hoax. The damage to the boat didn't match the report given by Dahl and Crisman. The debris ended up being ordinary aluminum slag. On August 3, Dahl and Crisman admitted to the hoax.

Returning home, Kenneth Arnold's single engine plane crashed. He survived but it was determined that the fuel valve had been purposely turned off. Weirder still, eleven days after Dahl and Crisman admitted to the hoax, reporter Paul Lantz died of unknown causes. Pathologists examined the Tacoma Times reporter's body for 36 hours but were unable to determine the cause of death.

FBI Director J. Edgar Hoover sent a teletype to agent George Wilcox on the day Lantz died, wherein Hoover said, "It would also appear that Dahl and Crisman did not admit the hoax to the army officers." Wilcox clarified the matter by noting, "Please be advised that Dahl did not admit to Brown that his story was a hoax but only stated that if questioned by authorities he was going to say it was a hoax because he did not want any further trouble over the matter." In fact, both Dahl and Crisman later recanted, claiming it was never a hoax.

Kenneth Arnold was understandably shaken. In a letter dated August 5, 1947, Palmer was forced to reassure Arnold that it OK to publish his investigation of the Maury Island affair.

> "I don't blame you for being alarmed, but I trust you've had no trouble in your flying since then. Let's get that straight—there's no horrible plot involved. It's probably true that the two men killed were just accidents. It could be true that it was not an accident, but I don't think there was any connection with the disks, or anything of that nature, nor is the material from Murray Island to blame.
>
> "Certainly I don't think you'd suffer from completing your report on your mission, and sending me your affidavit. Also, you'll have some money coming for that, and no sense to tossing that out of the window."

A Report of the Chicago Field Office of the FBI, dated September 20, 1947, drew further attention to

Palmer's hand in the fiasco:

> "...[I]t should be noted that [REDACTED for RAYMOND PALMER, ARNOLD]'s employer, was from the start "exploiting" the appearance of the flying discs, possibly to enhance the appeal of [REDACTED for SHAVER's] stories. It is possible, therefore, that the entire flying disc theory was conceived by [REDACTED, but probably RAYMOND PALMER]."

It seems unlikely that Ray Palmer invented the flying saucers. In the same letter to Kenneth Arnold mentioned above, Palmer himself noted that the phenomenon predated Arnold's 1947 sighting by several decades:

> "It is unfortunate that the thing seemed so big you had to call in army intelligence, but it will take them a long time to proceed to the point I've reached in this disk mystery. You see, you aren't the first to see them. They've been known for nearly forty years, and I have ample proof of that."

Whatever one thinks of the Maury Island affair, it planted the seeds for the idea of a government cover-up of UFO evidence, complete with the first tale of the Men in Black.

The fact that Kenneth Arnold and many other pilots and military personnel (i.e., credible witnesses) espoused the extraterrestrial hypothesis was compelling evidence for the public. The idea of extraterrestrial life had been around for a while. For example, in the 19th century, there was much speculation surrounding the intelligent origin of Martian "canals" described by Giovanni Schiaparelli and championed by Percival Lowell. Aliens were featured in comics, science fiction pulps and novels, and other media, including the infamous 1938 broadcast of *The War of the Worlds* by Orson Welles. Even so, according to Edward R. Murrow[2], the extraterrestrial hypothesis as a serious explanation did not earn serious attention until about 18 months after Kenneth Arnold's sighting.

Project Saucer

The Air Force began investigating flying saucers on July 9. 1947, leading to the formation of Project Sign (originally called Project Saucer) on January 22, 1948. Sign's purpose was to evaluate UFO reports to see if these flying saucers were a threat to national security. One of the concerns at the time was that the Soviets were building saucers, possibly with nuclear technology, with the aid of former Nazi scientists. We'd snagged Nazi rocket scientists like Dr. Wernher Von Braun through Operation Paperclip. We weren't stupid enough to believe that no one else had thought of the same idea.

The trouble was that saucer movements seemed to go well beyond the capabilities of known terrestrial capabilities. According to Ruppelt:

> "With the Soviets practically eliminated as a UFO source, the idea of interplanetary spaceships was becoming more popular. During 1948, the people in the Air Technical Intelligence Center (ATIC) were openly discussing the possibility of interplanetary visitors without others tapping their heads and looking smug.
>
> ... 'The Classics' were three historic reports that were the highlights of 1948. They are called 'The Classics,' a name given them by the Project Blue Book staff, because: (1) they are classic examples of how the true facts of a UFO report can be twisted and warped by some writers to prove their point, (2) they are the most highly publicized reports of this early era of the UFO's, and (3) they 'proved' to ATIC's intelligence specialists that UFO's were real.[3]"

The Classics

The Classics were the Thomas Mantell Crash of

January 7 (Franklin, KY), the Chiles-Whitted UFO encounter of July 24 (Montgomery, AL), and the Gorman UFO Dogfight of October 1 (Fargo, ND), 1948.

For those unfamiliar with these early UFO cases, which captivated the public's attention, here's a quick run-down.

On 7 January 1948, Kentucky Highway Patrol advised Godman Field at Fort Knox of a UFO near Maysville, Kentucky.

Sgt. Quinton Blackwell and two other witnesses saw the object from the control tower at Fort Knox at 1:45 PM. Four P-51 Mustangs of C Flight, 165th Fighter Squadron Kentucky Air National Guard, were ordered to pursue the UFO. One Mustang was low on fuel and had to pull out shortly. The remaining three pilots pursued the object at a steep climb. Lt. Albert Clements and Lt. Hammond discontinued the chase at 22,500 feet. Mantell continued to climb, but blacked out, presumably from lack of oxygen, after he passed 25,000 feet. His plane spiraled toward the ground until it crashed on a farm south of Franklin, Kentucky. Mantell's wristwatch stopped at 3:18 p.m., indicating the time of his crash.

The Mantell crash was reported by newspapers around the nation. A lot of misinformation was also circulated, including the idea that an alien spacecraft shot down Mantell's Mustang when he got too close.

The intense media attention put pressure on Project

Sign for a quick answer. They came up with Venus, an answer that never truly satisfied, mostly because Venus would have been little more than a "pinpoint of light" at the time. Later it was determined that the UFO was likely a Navy Skyhook weather balloon, Several were launched on 7 January 1948 in Clinton County, Ohio, approximately 150 miles (240 km) northeast of Fort Knox. Still, the Mantell case marked a shift in the media's attitude towards flying saucers. It seemed now that the stakes were higher.

At about 2:45 AM on July 24, 1948, Eastern Airlines pilot Clarence Chiles and his co-pilot, John Whitted, co-pilot, observed a glowing object as it flew past their Douglas DC-3 passenger plane near Montgomery, Alabama. Both men claimed that the object fly past the right side of their plane at a high rate of speed before it pulled "up with a tremendous burst of flame out of its rear and zoomed up into the clouds." They stated that the torpedo or cigar shaped UFO "looked like a wingless aircraft...it seemed to have two rows of windows through which glowed a very bright light, as brilliant as a magnesium flare." According to Ruppelt, the Chiles-Whitted report shook up military authorities worse than the Mantell incident, because "this was the first time two reliable sources had been really close enough to a UFO to get a good look and live to tell the tale.[4]"

The incident was originally listed as unexplained, but the fact was that the reliability of the witnesses was causing the investigators of Project Sign to come to a rather fantastic conclusion. Ruppelt notes:

> "In intelligence, if you have something to say about some vital problem you write a report that is known as an 'Estimate of the Situation.' A few days after the DC-3 was buzzed, the people at ATIC decided that the time had arrived to make an estimate of the Situation. The situation was the UFO's; the estimate was that they were interplanetary![5]"

Later skeptical investigations of the Chiles-Whitted UFO suggested that the Eastern Airlines flight had actually crossed paths with a fragmenting bolide. While the pilots vigorously disagreed with the meteor theory, but several things weigh in favorably for this solution. For starters, other than the basic shape, their drawings of the UFO were different. Whitted's drawing has a different front end from Chiles' rendition and sports a double row of six windows absent in the other's drawing. This suggests that their view of the UFO was subjective. A phenomenon known as the "airship effect" causes viewers to see fragmenting bolides (and other objects) as cigar-shaped craft with rows of windows. For example, on March 3, 1968, the Zond IV spacecraft reentered the atmosphere and broke up into a fireball. Despite knowing what it was, some folks still thought they saw a cigar-shaped craft with windows along the side.

A few days after Project Sign's "Estimate of the

Situation" was sent out, the third "Classic" UFO case occurred. Lt. George Gorman was participating in a cross-country flight with other National Guard pilots. On October 1, 1948, the other pilots decided to land at Fargo, North Dakota's Hector Airport, but Gorman stayed airborne in his P-51 Mustang for some night flying. Shortly after 9:00 PM, he noticed a strange blinking light. At 9:07, he called the control tower at Hector Airport and asked if there was any air traffic in the area other than his P-51 and a Piper Cub also visible at the time. The tower reported nothing but advised that the Piper pilot also saw a lighted object to the west.

Gorman gave chase. For 27 minutes, the veteran WWII fighter pilot pursued the light through a series of intricate maneuvers with more than one near collision. The "dogfight" (more of a game of tag) was witness by the two men in the Piper and the men in the control tower. The case became celebrated in the media.

Sign's official explanation for the round white object that Gorman pursued was that it was a lighted weather balloon. I know. I know, but in this case it's not that far-fetched. It turns out that the Air Weather Service released a lighted weather balloon from Fargo, ND, at 8:50 PM that night. It would have been in Gorman's air space by 9:00 PM.

Natural explanations aside, the Classics excited the imaginations of many, not only because of the sensational nature of the stories but also because credible witnesses were seeing UFOs and even interacting with them. More importantly, a good number of these witnesses believed, based on their observations of UFO movements and their conclusion that they defied present technological limits, that the things they were seeing were interplanetary in origin.

***

Notes

1. Clark, Jerome. *Strange Skies: Pilot Encounters with UFOs.* Citadel press (2003), p. 47.

2. Murrow, Edward R. "The Case of the Flying Saucer" CBS News. Radio broadcast. (April 7, 1950).

3. Ruppelt, Edward J. *The Report on Unidentified Flying Objects.* Victor Gollancz (1956), p. 30.

4. *Ibid.*, pp. 40-41.

5. Ibid., p. 41.

Tony Breeden

7 Trust No One

Not everyone appreciated Project Sign's enthusiasm for the extraterrestrial angle. Frankly, many thought it had strayed from its original objective. Sign's "Estimate of the Situation" was rejected by the USAF's Chief of Staff, General Hoyt Vandenberg for its espousal of the extraterrestrial hypothesis. Following the Chiles-Whitted sighting, Major General Charles P. Cabell requested that his Office of Air Intelligence, Defensive Analysis (AFOAI-DA) prepare a study examining "the possible tactics of the flying objects reported over the U.S."

On November 3, 1948, Cabell sent a letter with the subject line "Flying Object Incidents in the United States" demanding that Sign increase efforts to determine whether these objects were domestic or foreign in origin. Colonel McCoy responded in a letter dated five days afterward, in which he defended Sign's methods and summarized their current findings. Among those finding was the remark that "the discs, cigar shaped objects and 'balls of light' are not of domestic origin." Noting that modern technology was insufficient to account for the observed movements of UFOs, he re-iterated that "The possibility that the reported objects are vehicles from another planet has not been ignored." While McCoy admitted that tangible evidence for the interplanetary hypothesis was "completely lacking" and even noted that "the exact nature of those objects cannot be established until physical evidence, such as that which would result from a crash, has been obtained," he referenced "The Books of Charles

Fort" as evidence that this phenomenon predated the modern era.

Cabell was apparently unimpressed with the Forteans at Project Sign. The AFOAI's December 10, 1948 report, entitled "Analysis of Flying Object Incidents in the U.S.," considered only the domestic and foreign origins of UFOs. Predictably, they determined that the Soviets were the most likely foreign source of these aircraft.

Sign's final report was issued in February 1949. An Appendix prepared by Dr. James E. Lipp of Project Rand said this about the extraterrestrial hypothesis:

"It is hard to believe that any technically accomplished race would come here, flaunt its ability in mysterious ways and then simply go away... The lack of purpose apparent in the various episodes is also puzzling. Only one motive can be assigned; that the spacemen are "feeling out" our defenses without wanting to be belligerent. If so, they must have been satisfied long ago that we can't catch them. It seems fruitless for them to keep repeating the same experiment. Conclusions: Although visits from outer space are believed to be possible, they are believed to be very improbable. In particular, the actions attributed to the 'flying objects' reported during 1947 and 1948 seem inconsistent with the requirements for space travel."

Project Grudge

Project Sign was replaced by Project Grudge on February 11, 1949. Grudge existed primarily as a public relations agency to explain away UFO sightings as mundane and ordinary phenomena. Air Force Captain Edward J. Ruppelt, who later headed Project Blue Book in its early years, criticized Grudge, writing that "Everything was being evaluated on the premise that UFOs couldn't exist. No matter what you see or hear, don't believe it[1]." He characterized it as the "Dark Ages" of Air Force UFO investigation.

Grudge made the Air Force's new position clear in a two part *Saturday Evening Post* article by Sidney Shallet called "What You Can Believe About Flying Saucers" (April 30, 1949 & May 7, 1949). The article stated that the flying saucer phenomenon had been blown out of proportion by the press, that most sightings were explainable by mundane causes, and that hoaxes and crackpots accounted for the rest.

The 600-plus-page Grudge Report of August 1949 (its only official report), concluded that:

> "A. There is no evidence that objects reported upon are the result of an advanced scientific foreign

development; and, therefore they constitute no direct threat to the national security. In view of this, it is recommended that the investigation and study of reports of unidentified flying objects be reduced in scope. Headquarters AMC Air Material Command will continue to investigate reports in which realistic technical applications are clearly indicated.

NOTE: It is apparent that further study along present lines would only confirm the findings presented herein. It is further recommended that pertinent collection directives be revised to reflect the contemplated change in policy.

B. All evidence and analyses indicate that reports of unidentified flying objects are the result of:

1. Misinterpretation of various conventional objects.

2. A mild form of mass-hysteria and war nerves.

3. Individuals who fabricate such reports to perpetrate a hoax or to seek publicity.

4. Psychopathological persons."

The report admitted that 23% of the 244 cases it had investigated were unexplainable with the caveat that they believed there were "sufficient psychological explanations" that could account for those as-yet-unexplained accounts. It's primary concern with flying discs was the fear that UFO reports might be used to overwhelm communications during a Soviet attack or for psychological warfare purposes, especially to create mass hysteria, like Orson Welles' 1938 radio broadcast of *The War of the Worlds* had allegedly achieved.

In late December, radio commentator Frank Edwards received an advance copy of a forthcoming *True* magazine article by a retired Marine Corps aviator named Major Donald Keyhoe. The article was called, "Flying Saucers Are Real." Realizing it would be a sensation, Edwards hounded *True* editor Ken Purdy for permission to tell the public about it and started doing so on about December 21, 1949 and thereafter. The press picked up his enthusiasm, basically guaranteeing its success that when the article was finally published December 26, 1949.

Almost immediately, the Air Force responded quickly to deny the *True* magazine article. The very next day, it announced that Project Saucer had been ordered ended because there was nothing to indicate that UFOs were "not the results of natural phenomena." They claimed that all evidence pointed to three factors: "misinterpretation of various conventional objects; a mild form of mass hysteria;

or hoaxes."

Truth be told, Keyhoe's influential "Flying Saucers Are Real," was sparked by contradictions between the April Project Saucer press memorandum and the April 30th & May 7th *Washington Post* articles by Sidney Shallet. Ken Purdy of *True* magazine recruited Keyhoe to investigate the flying saucer enigma. Purdy was convinced that the saucers were a cover-up for something bigger. Keyhoe later wrote that Ken Purdy explained:

> "There's something damned queer going on. For fifteen months, `Project Saucer' is buttoned up tight. Top Secret. Then suddenly, Forrestal gets the Saturday Evening Post to run two articles, brushing the whole thing off. The first piece hits the stands – and what happens?"

> "The same day, the Air Force rushes out this `Project Saucer' report. It admits they haven't identified the disks in any important cases. They say it's still serious enough – wait a minute –' he thumbed through the stapled papers – 'to require constant vigilance by Project `Saucer' personnel and civilian population.'[2]"

In other words, while the *Post* assured the public that flying saucers were no concern, the press memorandum stated that flying saucers "are not a joke" and suggested that the situation was still far from settled. The other glaring contradiction between the two publications concerned with the official explanation for the Mantell case. The *Post* stated the Air Force's explanation of the UFO as Venus, qualified with the possibility that it was a weather balloon. The press memorandum said the object was unexplained. Purdy was convinced that UFOs were a cover-up for something bigger.

Keyhoe's article and the resulting press coverage basically un-did everything Grudge's propaganda campaign hoped to accomplish. Even the announced end of Grudge, a rather heavy-handed tactic, seemed to fuel media suspicions of a cover-up. The article's very first conclusion was that "For the past 175 years, the planet Earth has been under systematic close-range examination by living, intelligent observers from another planet." Worse still, from the government's point of view, Keyhoe not only became a crusader for the extraterrestrial hypothesis, he greatly helped to popularize the idea of a government conspiracy to cover up the truth about flying saucers.

In January 1950, *Time* magazine, *Variety*, and various newspapers began reporting rumors of a crashed saucer from Venus being held by the government in secret. Other pro-extraterrestrial articles began appearing in *True* and other magazines as the year went on. By year's end, Keyhoe had published a book called *The Flying Saucers Are Real*, expanding the material in his *True* article and giving the extraterrestrial hypothesis and the idea of a government cover-up of UFOs a wider audience.

Another popular UFO book, *Behind the Flying Saucers* by Frank Scully, also hit the market in 1950. This one concerned an alleged saucer crash in Aztec, New Mexico in March 1948. Scully had written about the crash in his Variety column in October and November 1949, claiming that the Aztec saucer, its dead little alien pilots and other craft from Venus were being held by the government.

In January 1951, Bob Considine wrote an article in *Cosmopolitan* magazine called "The Disgraceful Flying Saucer Hoax!" Infamously believed to be a propaganda piece by Grudge, it was the first publication to admit that "Project Saucer" was still around despite the announcement to the contrary. In the article, Constantine claimed:

> "Pranksters, half-wits, cranks, publicity hounds, and fanatics in general are having the time of their lives playing on the gullibility and Cold War jitters of the average citizen. It is their malicious fancy to populate the skies over America with a vessel that just does not exist — the flying saucer."

In support, the article cast doubt on Scully's claims

and sources in *Behind the Flying Saucers*. The article concluded with several quotes from Lt. Col. Harold E. Watson, chief of the Air Tactical Intelligence Center (ATIC) at Wright Patterson Air Force Base, who lamented that Scully's book "made me slightly ill after fifteen pages."

At the time, Grudge basically consisted of Lt. Col. Watson and Grudge's head, Lt. James Rodgers, and Lt. Gerry Cummings. Watson's final estimation of the situation was:

> "There are no flying saucers, no 'little men,' no burned saucer wreckage or pieces of flying saucers, no disappearing parachutists, no potential enemy with any craft of this sort, and none of our own design.
>
> "There just ain't no such animal, but tracking down the nonexistent cause of mass hysteria is still costing us — and you — plenty."

In April 1951, Bob Ginna of *Life* magazine paid a visit to Wright-Patterson. When he spoke to the Project Saucer staff, he found them disorganized and largely ignorant of their supposed field of expertise. Several obviously anti-saucer personnel were reassigned in response to the reporter's findings.

The final blow for Grudge's era of indifference came on September 10, 1951 when a student operator at the

Army Signals Corps radar center at Fort Monmouth, NJ, picked up an unknown object moving too fast to be tracked automatically. This occurred during a demonstration to visiting Air Force officers. A dull silver, disc-like object was sighted a half hour later by Lt. Wilbert Rogers and Maj. Edward Ballard as they were flying over Point Pleasant, NJ. The next day, Fort Monmouth radar picked up more UFOs that could not be tracked automatically. Cummings and Rodgers at Grudge disagreed over the validity of the Fort Monmouth sightings. After a call to General Cabell, Cummings went to New Jersey to investigate with another officer, and then afterward Washington DC to brief Cabell. Cummings reported that every UFO sighting was taken as a huge joke by Watson and Rodgers and that the only "analysis" consisted of Rodgers trying to think up new and original explanations that hadn't been sent to Washington before.

Cabell was furious.

Blue Book

General Cabell reorganized Grudge and put Captain Edward Ruppelt in charge. The entire tone of the Air Force's investigation of UFOs changed. Cabell demanded more open-mindedness and insisted that research techniques be updated to be more scientific. They were also to re-assess the old Grudge reports.

In March 1952, the project's name was officially changed to Blue Book. The April 1952 issue of *Life* magazine featured an eye-catching cover photo of

Marilyn Monroe. It also carried an article by Bob Ginna and H.B. Darrach Jr called "Have We Visitors From Outer Space?" It outlined several UFO cases and stated the Air Force's new policy in which it "invites all citizens to report their sightings to the nearest Air Force installation. All reports will be given expert consideration and those of special interest will be thoroughly investigated. The identity of those making such reports will be kept in confidence; no one will be ridiculed for making one." More significantly, the article all but endorsed the possibility, if not the probability of the extraterrestrial hypothesis.

Perhaps it is no coincidence that also in April 1952, Albert K. Bender, science fiction, rocketry, and newly converted saucer fan, founded the International Flying Saucer Bureau (IFSB) in Bridgeport, Connecticut. He and his fellow saucerians had much to hold their attention in the months to come.

In July 1952, a UFO flap occurred, the largest to date, culminating in sightings in Washington D.C. Some folks were seeing bright lights that coincided with radar detections. Blue Book decided that the radar reports were due to temperature inversions, but the media had a field day. The CIA became very concerned.

Meanwhile, things continued to stay interesting for the saucerians. August 19, 1952 brought the Sonny Desverges case where in a UFO somehow allegedly burned a hole in a scoutmaster's cap. The IFSB swelled to 100 members in 16 states. On September 10, 1952, *People Today* magazine featured an article by its editors called "Flying Saucers Are Real," which claimed that UFOs were really just ultrasonic guided missiles built by both the US and the USSR. Also in September, an article in *True* magazine by J.P. Cahn entitled, "The Flying Saucers and the Mysterious Little Men," proved that that the tale told of a crashed saucer in Aztec, NM, in Frank Scully's *Behind the Flying Saucers* (1950) was a hoax by two con men who had likewise duped Scully.

September 12, 1952 made headlines with the Flatwoods Monster of Braxton County, WV, an alleged case of a close encounter of the third kind. This case marked the first foray into the UFO field by West Virginia native Gray Barker, who turned the headlines into an opportunity to write a story for Ray Palmer's *Fate* magazine. The first issue of *Space Review*, the newsletter of Albert Bender's IFSB, was published in October. The following month, Gray Barker saw an advertisement for the IFSB in Ray Palmer's *Other Worlds* magazine. Barker wrote to Bender on November 20, 1952, offering his help. By January 1953, Barker had become a member of the IFSB and the representative for West Virginia. His story on the Flatwoods Monster, "The Monster and the Saucer," was featured in *Fate* magazine that same month. Impressed, Albert Bender named Barker as the Chief Investigator of the IFSB's new investigative team.

The Robertson Panel

Unfortunately, there were things going on behind the scenes that the IFSB and other private saucer organizations knew nothing about. Most notably, the CIA sponsored "Robertson Panel" was convened on January 14-17, 1953. The Panel's report concluded UFOs could be explained as terrestrial phenomena and that UFOs were not a direct threat to national security; however, they worried that "related dangers might well exist resulting from:

> a. Misidentification of actual enemy artifacts by defense personnel.
>
> b. Overloading of emergency reporting channels with 'false' information.
>
> c. Subjectivity of public to mass hysteria and greater vulnerability to possible enemy psychological warfare."

Among their recommendations were an education program partly consisting of a "debunking aim" which would "result in reduction in public interest in 'flying saucers' which today evokes a strong psychological reaction. This education could be accomplished by mass media such as television, motion pictures, and popular articles. Basis of such education would be actual case histories which had been puzzling at first but later explained. As in the case of conjuring tricks, there is much less stimulation if the 'secret' is known."

The Panel also took note of private flying saucer groups and recommended that "such organizations should be watched because of their potentially great influence on mass thinking if widespread sightings should occur. The apparent irresponsibility and the possible use of such groups for subversive purposes should be kept in mind."

Men in Black

Which brings us back to the International Flying Saucer Bureau. The IFSB was perhaps the largest private saucer organization in existence at the time. At its height, the IFSB had branches in all 49 States of the U.S. and the District of Columbia (Hawaii was not yet a state), Puerto Rico, Canada, the UK, France, Australia and New Zealand. It had the likes of WWI flying ace Eddie Rickenbacker on its honorary membership roll, and such luminaries as Robert N Webster (aka Raymond E. Palmer of *Fate* magazine, etc.), Meade Layne of the Borderland Sciences Research Association, and Coral Lorenzen (co-founder and President of the Aerial Phenomena Research Organization (APRO)) on its honorary international board of directors.

Yet in the October 1953 issue of *Space Review*, at the height of its apparent success, Albert Bender announced the end of the IFSB. It was a shock to everyone in the saucerian community, to say the least.

The last issue of *Saucer News* included a "Late Bulletin":

> "A source which the IFSB considers very reliable has informed us that the investigation of the flying saucer mystery and the solution is approaching final stages. This same source to whom we had referred data, which had come into our possession, suggested that it was not the proper method and time to publish the data in Space Review."

There was also a mysterious "Statement of Importance":

> "The mystery of the flying saucers is no longer a mystery. The source is already known, but any information about this is being withheld by order from a higher source. We would like to print the full story in Space Review, but because of the nature of the information we are very sorry that we have been advised in the negative."

The statement ended in the sentence "We advise those engaged in saucer work to please be very cautious."

Queries by Barker and other members of the IFSB were stonewalled by Bender. Then suddenly the Bridgeport, CT *Sunday Herald* carried a story by Lem M'Collum on Bender in its November 11, 1953 edition, entitled, "Mystery Visitors Halt Research: Saucerers Here Ordered To Quit." According to the article:

> "Bender said 'three men wearing dark suits' came to his home, flashed credentials showing them to be members of the 'higher authority' …and told him 'not roughly, but sternly and emphatically' to stop publishing flying saucer information."

The saucerian world immediately began speculating on who this "higher authority" was and why Bender had shut down the IFSB. Coral Lorenzen suggested that Bender had lost the financial backing of an important member of the IFSB and was trying to get out of the saucering business before his bankruptcy became inevitable. Some thought it might have something to do a fireball that punched a hole through a metal signboard in New Haven, CT on August 19, 1953. IFSB investigator August "Augie" Roberts was on the scene and took a sample of the metal from the sign right under the noses of Navy ordnance investigators. Certainly, the IFSB's trouble began at that point. Bender had the fragment sent off to the IFSB's newly appointed Chief Research Consultant, retired Army Colonel Robert B.

Emerson, to be tested at Emerson Testing Laboratories (Baton Rouge, LA).

On August 28, 1953, Barker claimed to have received a visit from the FBI. Another member of Bender's investigative team, Rev. S.L. Daw, received a separate visit. Both sent letters to Bender, who was away at the time. It's worth mentioning that neither FBI visit included questions about the New Haven incident or even the Flatwoods Monster incident, which both parties had independently investigated.

David Houchin[3], curator of the Gray Barker Collection in Clarksburg, WV, is on record suggesting that Barker's FBI visit might have had nothing to do with saucering at all – nothing beside the fact that one of his IFSB Chief Investigator business card was found in the pocket of a young Florida service man at St. Mary's Hospital in Clarksburg, WV. The young man had been brought in after an epileptic seizure and the FBI came knocking on Barker's door to see what he could tell them about the man, whose name Barker says he forgot. Barker was a closeted homosexual and, according to Houchin, he liked to pick up young men for that purpose and perhaps he tried to impress the fellow with his business card. In any case, since homosexual acts were illegal at the time, it is perhaps understandable that Barker might feign ignorance concerning the fellow and his involvement with him. On a practical level, Houchin's theory would mean that Barker's FBI visit was unrelated to the IFSB's shutdown.

When he returned, Bender was alarmed at the news and later said he received his own visit from "men in black suits and Homburgs." Bender also claimed that he felt he had solved the mystery of the flying saucers. Bender wrote down his theory and sent it off to a friend in Washington, D.C. whom he felt he could trust. When the three men appeared at Bender's door, one of them held that letter in his hand. They confirmed that he'd solved the saucer mystery but then scared him into silence. Fellow IFSB investigator Dominic Lucchessi stated in a taped correspondence to Gray Barker that Bender was "pledged to secrecy, on his honor as an American citizen not to speak about the actual thing that he knew.[4]"

The Rev. S.L. Daw's FBI visit may or may not have had much to do with the IFSB's shutdown. It's possible that Daw was the friend in DC to whom Bender sent his saucer theory and that this brought on Daw's FBI visit. Daw was also known to take saucer photographs near military bases, which could have brought him trouble with the authorities independently of his affiliations with the IFSB. On September 9, 1953, Bender sent Daw a letter in which he expressed his fears concerning the cause of the FBI visits (according to a handwritten copy sent from Daw to Barker):

> "It certainly must be over the mention of installations that caused all the concern. It certainly

> was too bad that Mr. Lucchesi was
> so careless in handling the
> information for our bureau."

In *They Knew Too Much About Flying Saucers,* Barker claimed that the probable identity of the document lost by Lucchesi was a photo analysis of an alleged UFO by Mark A. Curilovic, which was ultimately rejected as an optical illusion. It was later discovered that someone had turned it in to the police after which it was recovered, with some miscommunications on both sides. Barker found the matter strange but admitted that the Curilovic matter could have absolutely nothing to do with the FBI visits.

Barker transcribed an April 1954 telephone conversation which also mentions these installations Bender refers to:

> BARKER: It is my impression that they lost that report in New Jersey and they found it, and became curious about the organization. At the time I thought because you said something about a gun emplacement.
>
> DAW: That's what it was, there, because, I know that sport.
>
> BARKER: You do?
>
> DAW: Yeah.

BARKER: You've been there?

DAW: Oh, my yes.

BARKER: Are cameras allowed there?

DAW: No!

So it would appear that the report in question either pictured or mentioned gun emplacements at a location Rev. Daw stated no cameras were allowed. Did the report concern a photograph of a possible UFO near a military installation? Was the fireball that punched a hole in that signboard from a gun emplacement that the military didn't want attention called to? If so, the report could have garnered the attention of the FBI all on its own.

Or did the report concern Bender's "Project X"? Bender launched Project X with members of the IFSB's Australian and New Zealand branches to chart the path of UFOs to determine their point of origin. If the UFOs reported were actually military craft and showed the locations of bases, one could see why US military officials might get a bit concerned.

And it's also possible that the IFSB had been on the government's radar since shortly after the Robertson Panel. You see, according to FBI FOIA files, someone from the Department of Civil Defense in Johnson County, Franklin, Indiana wrote the FBI, asking if the IFSB "is cleared or is subversive in any way." The anonymous informant also included the current issue (January 1953) of Space Review, which includes an article by Rev. S. L Daw connecting the Flatwoods incident with a possible secret lunar lander akin to the one shown in Collier's magazine's "Man Will Conquer Space Soon!" series. It also names a lot of the IFSB's state representatives (including Gray Barker) and demonstrated their international scope. Ironically, it also featured an article about the formation of a Franklin, Indiana chapter of the IFSB after the town joined pretty much *en masse* after a wave of UFO sightings. The article mentions a "Mr. Robert Wolf, civil defense director" as being one of those instrumental in the success of the formation of the Franklin, Indiana chapter. Of course, it's possible that someone else in his department queried the FBI, but the fact remains that the IFSB was on the government's radar within a week of the Robertson Panel's warning that civilian saucer groups were to be watched.

My personal theory is that the IFSB just experienced a perfect storm of unrelated attention from the authorities, but at a level that poor Bender considered too much! The FBI knew about the IFSB shortly after the Robertson Panel recommended keeping an eye on these civilian saucer groups. Augie Roberts grabbed a fragment from under the noses of Naval Ordnance investigators, which Bender sent to be tested by a retired Army Colonel. Dominic Lucchesi lost a document that contained either photographs or details about gun emplacements in an area, likely military, where photography was not allowed. S.L. Daw and Barker both receive FBI visits. Bender allegedly receives one of his own, and he's been working with international members to map out the movement of aerial objects in the Pacific. This was the day of McCarthyism and J. Edgar Hoover. It's possible that the whole line about being silenced on his honor as an American citizen was simply a shout-out to the powers-that-be that he was surrendering and that he was not a Communist threat.

Gray Barker spent the next several years investigating the "Bender Mystery." In 1956, he wrote a book called *They Knew Too Much About Flying Saucers*. Barker tied in the Maury Island affair, the IFSB shutdown and several other "Men in Black" incidents to suggest a conspiracy against Ufologists who were silenced for getting too close to the truth.

Capitalizing on Keyhoe's "Silence group," Barker suggested that the Men in Black were government agents or possibly something even more fantastic! In time, the Men in Black became a mainstay of saucer conspiracy lore and worked their way into the public consciousness. A 2012 Kelton Research survey of a random sample of 1114 Americans adults found that 55 percent of those surveyed believe that real Men in Black are actually trying to silence UFO researchers.

It has to be said that, according to his good friend Jim Moseley, Gray Barker had lost his faith in saucers by the time he wrote *They Knew Too Much About Flying Saucers*. He was known to fabricate some of his stories, so it's hard to say how much of his book is actually true. Still, over the next several decades, the government would reveal, bit by bit, that it was indeed covering things up... just nothing to do with flying saucers.

Confirmed Government Cover-ups

National security comes with an obligate level of secrecy and misdirection when it comes to top secret military projects. We've already mentioned how some flying saucers, especially "crashed saucer" debris like that found in Roswell, NM, were likely misidentified Project Mogul balloons or hybrid aircraft that were classified and therefore ineligible as an explanation even if it happened to be true. Likewise, Operation Dive, a secret 1950s Air Force project which tested high-altitude parachutes using anthropomorphic dummies, likely accounts for tales of alien bodies recovered at "crash sites" and being whisked away by the government thereafter; that is, *if* Redfern is wrong about that more disturbing possibility we mentioned.

In 1997, historian Gerald K. Haines wrote a research paper for *Studies in Intelligence* called "The CIA's Role in the Study of UFOs, 1947-90" in which he noted:

> "According to later estimates from CIA officials who worked on the U-2 project and the OXCART (SR-71, or Blackbird) project, over half of all UFO reports from the late 1950s through the 1960s were

accounted for by manned reconnaissance flights (namely the U-2) over the United States. This led the Air Force to make misleading and deceptive statements to the public in order to allay public fears and to protect an extraordinarily sensitive national security project. While perhaps justified, this deception added fuel to the later conspiracy theories and the cover up controversy of the 1970s."

SR-71s and their predecessor, the A-12, are capable of a maneuver called a "dipsy doodle." Basically, the pilot noses the aircraft over at about 33,000 feet with the plane at Mach .95, then dives for 10 to 20 seconds at around a 30 degree pitch 30 degrees, and finally accelerates skyward at more than twice the speed of sound. This maneuver accounts for a UFOs ability to swoop downward, apparently hover and then soar into the sky at impossible speeds.

The existence of Area 51 (aka Groom Lake) has been categorically denied by the US government until 2013, when the CIA released documents that proved not only the existence but the location of the facility. Unfortunately, despite sci-fi film portrayals and conspiracy theories to the contrary, Area 51 contains no extraterrestrial craft or corpses. It was a top secret research facility that, among other things, helped develop the U-2 spy plane.

We could go on with instances where the government has finally revealed a secret project that was misidentified as UFO sightings, but that wouldn't be fair. You see, the shadier side of the coin is that the government has also been known to cover up legitimate research with saucer-laced lies.

Whether true or not, in letters to Gray Barker and Jim Moseley, contactee Howard Menger claimed that his book, *From Outer Space To You* [1959], was "fact-fiction" and that after he sent his UFO pictures to the Pentagon, the US government had asked him to cooperate in an experiment to gauge the public's reaction to extraterrestrial contact. He later recanted his hoax claim, but of course he was trying to sell his new book.

On the same vein, Dr. Leon Davidson, the self-same fellow who once upon a time convinced a Congressional Committee to force the Air Force to permit him to publish and distribute Project Blue Book's *Special Report No. 14*, claimed that some of contactee George Adamski's contacts were set up by the CIA and that UFOs were a hoax perpetrated by same.

The best known example concerns Richard Doty, a special agent with the US Air Force Office of Special Investigations (AFOSI), who so convinced retired WWII veteran Paul Bennewitz of an alien conspiracy that he was institutionalized for paranoia. The reason Bennewitz was targeted was because he came forward with what he believed to be evidence of UFOs flying around Kirtland Air Force Base. In actuality, he was picking up evidence of covert government projects. Doty made an asset of Ufologist William Moore, co-author (with Charles Berlitz) of *The Philadelphia Experiment* (1979) and *The Roswell Incident*, promising to tell him what the government knew about UFOs in return for his cooperation. Doty fed fake evidence to Bennewitz, including government documents delivered through Moore. One of those forged documents was the "Aquarius Document" (also known as the "NASA [or NSA] Telex"), which also happens to be the first time anyone ever read of "MJ Twelve." This is just one of many, many reasons the MJ-12 documents are bogus.

Coming full circle, I would be remiss if I did not mention the fact that Kenneth Arnold's original sighting bears a significant resemblance to a crescent shaped Horten Brothers craft like the *Parabola*. If Nick Redfern's theory about experimental prototypes based on the *Parabola* design being tested in the United States is true, they could account for not only the Roswell crash but also Arnold's original sensational report.

The bottom line is that the conspiracy theories about government cover ups aren't completely unfounded; however, that doesn't mean that alien bodies and craft are locked away in some hangar or underground government base. The real answer is likely to be more mundane, if fantastic in its own right.

***

Notes

1. Ruppelt, Edward J. *The Report on Unidentified Flying Objects*. Victor Gollancz (1956), p. 60.

2. Keyhoe, Donald. "Flying Saucers Are Real." *Fawcett Publications* (1950), pp. 18-19.

3. "Inside the Mind of Gray Barker." *Exploring the Bizarre with Timothy Green Beckley and Tim Schwartz*. Guests: Allen Greenfield, Steve Ward and David Houchin. KCORRadio.com. Web. Aired January 28, 2016. MP3. Retrieved October 10, 2016.

4. Barker, Gray. *They Knew Too Much About Flying Saucers*. University Press (1956), p.114.

Tony Breeden

8 Unidentified Lying Saucers

Anecdotal evidence for the UFO phenomenon comes in the form of thousands of photos and videos of alleged flying saucers, and eyewitness accounts, some of which come from highly credible folk like US Presidents, NASA astronauts and military personnel. These people are sincere in their beliefs that they are seeing and experiencing something real. It is also undeniable that the UFO landscape is littered with outright hoaxes and frauds.

On this wise, the credulity of the UFO field is rather breath-taking! It makes sorting through the puzzle just that more difficult, because folks tend to just uncritically pass along those things that conform to their beliefs. Speculation from one Ufologist becomes gospel truth in the next investigator's telling.

For example, writing of Warren Smith, a West Virginia born author of fiction and Fortean non-fiction, Kevin Randle noted that:

> "Smith made up stuff when he needed to add detail or credibility to a story. He seemed to think nothing of this. He thought it was part of doing business as a writer of the unusual and paranormal. If you didn't have what you needed, why you just invented it.
>
> "Others, following Smith, then quoted his published work,

assuming that some kind of vetting process had taken place. They believed that Smith wouldn't have made it up and that if the facts didn't check out, well then, the fact checkers at the publisher would catch them and correct them. The sad truth is that many publishers don't care what the facts are as long as the book is interesting and the public will buy it. Cash in the pocket is the bottom line and truth has nothing to do with it.[1]"

The reason that no one bothers with fact-checking to any great extent or conducts critical investigation is because often the entire thing is an exercise in confirmation bias. And that criticism applies whether one is a saucerian or a skeptic!

I'm not the only one to note this. The late Jim Moseley, alternately called the Supreme Commander and Reigning Court Jester of Ufology, noted a disturbing yet prevalent aspect of the UFO culture that he termed Saucer Logic which boils down to the credulous use of obvious logical fallacies to force all pegs of whatever shape into a saucer-shaped hole. The only consistency to Saucer Logic is one's predetermined conclusion. For example, the field sees a conspiracy when the government doesn't release information or, conversely, when it releases information that doesn't confirm their particular saucer theory.

Consider the case of Tom Monteleone. Before he became a sci-fi author, Tom garnered attention in the UFO community when he called in to Fred Gale's show on Washington DC's WWDC radio station in December 1967. On this particular show, Gale was interviewing a man from the Parkersburg, WV area by the name of Woodrow "Woody" Derenberger.

Derenberger claimed that on November 2, 1966 at approximately 7:25 PM, while en route I-77 from Marietta, Ohio to his home in Mineral Wells, WV, his truck was stopped by a space vehicle just before the Route 47 intersection (aka Exit 174/Staunton Avenue). The 50 year old sewing machine salesman claimed that the charcoal colored vehicle was shaped "like an old-fashioned kerosene lamp chimney, flaring at both ends, narrowing down to a small neck and then enlarging in a great bulge in the center." A human-looking figure in an overcoat with dark hair and tan skin stepped out of the craft, walked up to Derenberger's truck and said, "Do not be afraid. We mean you no harm. I come from a country much less powerful than yours."

Derenberger maintained that the grinning man spoke to him telepathically, without moving his lips. They had an odd, but brief telepathic conversation, in which the stranger introduced himself as "Cold" and promised the dumbstruck Derenberger that "We will see you again." Cold also told Derenberger to tell the authorities of his encounter and that he would come forward to confirm the story later. Afterward, Cold walked back to his vehicle. An unseen figure opened the door for Cold and then the ship took off vertically.

When he got home, Derenberger called the authorities as he'd been instructed. The next day, he held a press conference and was interviewed by Thomas Barker and Ronald Maines for WTAP television and radio. During the interview, Maines, general manager of WTAP, noted that during one of the recent broadcasts of the Joe Pyne TV Show the host had interviewed a man who had "taken things one step further and he had been taken aboard a spaceship" which Maines noted "was described quite similarly" to the ship Derenberger had described. Those aliens also looked like humans, which was pretty typical for alien encounters during the 50s and 60s, and they took him to Venus and then Mars.

As fate would have it, Derenberger was contacted by Cold again the very next day on his way home from Pomeroy, Ohio. Cold's ship stayed directly over the human's vehicle and, as before, Cold communicated telepathically – which I suppose explains why Derenberger's passenger, Philip Elliot of Parkersburg, neither saw nor heard anything during the encounter. Well, except for seeing that Derenberger appeared to be in some sort of a trance. This was kind of a big deal because Derenberger was driving at the time! Somehow Elliot managed to keep them from having an accident and take notes all at the same time. During the telepathic trance, Derenberger was told that Cold's first name was

Indrid and that he was from the planet Lanulos in the Ganymede galaxy. One of their legends said that the Lanulosians were from Earth originally. As Derenberger wrote in the November 1968 issue of *Probe*[2,3]:

> "They believe their forefathers came from Earth in a space ship and after they had landed, somehow lost the art of space travel. It was many, many years before they again learned how to travel in space."

Like us, Lanulosians believed in one God, the creator of all good things. Theirs was a world without strife and war; in fact, they had no word for hate. Time on Lanulos works differently from Earth time, so that Cold and his associates had to make their visits brief if they didn't want to grow too young to recall how to operate their spacecraft!

Later the next year, Cold and his alien navigator Carl Ardo would take return to take Woody on board their space ship, and they would visit his home planet of Lanulos, which turned out to be, as John Keel[4] put it, "a pleasant little planet where the people ran around nearly nude." Incidentally, Derenberger later found out first-hand, or so he claimed, that Venus was likewise populated *sans* clothing.

Contactees who seem to develop on-going relationships with the space people are known as UFO repeaters. Gray Barker wrote about the repeater phenomenon in the *Book of Adamski* (1967):

> "Something real, though weird and fantastic, happens to an individual and he tells the world about it. People come from miles around to hear the story, and then want to hear more. ...The saucer 'contactee' may similarly concoct further accounts, not wishing to disappoint his public.[5]"

Or as he put it in an interview later:

> "Some of their follow-up stories aren't very believable.[6]"

In the meantime, Derenberger's fame had a cost. He was deluged with letters and telephone calls. People would line up along the road to his farm, even sitting in the trees[7], armed with guns, hoping to catch a glimpse of a saucer – and presumably to provoke an interstellar war!

This part of the story has always amused me, partly because Derenberger's wife[8] is quoted as saying:

> "They [the aliens] aren't making contact only around here. They are doing this all over the country. But they find the people in West Virginia more receptive."

A friend of mine in high school had the exact opposite opinion, which he usually conveyed via an imagined conversation between two shotgun-toting rednecks leaning on a fence:

> "Wazzat?"
>
> "I think it's a spaceship."
>
> "Should we shoot it?"
>
> "Yup."

In any case, even after the Derenbergers moved a few times and switched to an unlisted number, they began receiving threatening phone calls from people telling him to shut up about his story. Eventually, his wife and kids moved out of the area, partly to escape the harassment and partly because Woodrow Derenberger was two-timing his wife[9]. He moved away in December 1967 after their divorce and married a much younger fellow contactee[10]. Conversely, his ex-wife married a UFO researcher from Cleveland, Ohio[11].

There was also what John Keel referred to as an "absurd rumor[12]": that Woodrow Derenberger was pregnant with a half-alien child who was destined to be a world leader. Some versions even suggest that Cold was the baby daddy!

I haven't even got to the good part of this bizarre story. There were already a lot of reasons to doubt Derenberger's tales of visitors from a nudist planet. One of the more glaring problems with his yarn is that Ganymede isn't a galaxy at all; it's one of Jupiter's moons. We also know that Venus, which he likewise claimed to have visited, is way too hot to support life.

Another problem was that no one was seeing these aliens or ships but him. Oh, Keel claims that when he and Gray Barker[13] went to investigate Derenberger's claims about four months after Indrid Cold's first visit, they saw some strange lights hovering over a field near his house. When they went to get a closer look, they found the fence around the property was electrified. Keel got a nasty shock and had to fend off an ill-tempered bull! Having watched Keel get blown over the decidedly hostile fence, Barker wisely decided not to brave either the fence or the bull.

Walter Vanscoy[14], an independent eyewitness to Derenberger's first encounter with Indrid Cold could only state that he saw him pulled alongside the road talking to a man in an overcoat. The spaceship was nowhere to be seen.

When Monteleone first made himself known on Fred Gale's call-in show, he declared that he knew Derenberger's story was real because he'd been to Lanulos too! At the time, Monteleone gave the name Ed Bailey but refused to give anything other than the name because he claimed he didn't want any publicity. That sentiment apparently didn't last long. After being contacted by Harold Salkin, Derenberger's manager, Monteleone admitted his true identity and the fact that he was a 21 year old psychology major at the University of Maryland.

A week or so later, Salkin and the Derenbergers

taped an interview with Monteleone, in which he stated that at 1 AM on December 10, 1967, he had been stopped on the interstate by a UFO, pretty much like Derenberger. Like the other Lanulosian contactee, he had a chat with a human looking alien, although his name was Vadig. Vadig ended the conversation by saying, "I'll see you in time." Two months later, Vadig returned and shortly after he took Monteleone to the lovely nudist planet of Lanulos. At the end of the trip, Vadig once again said, "I will see you in time." There had been two more brief visits since then.

John Keel came to interview Monteleone in late March 1967. In the *Mothman Prophecies*, Keel said, "Naturally, I suspected the whole thing was some kind of put-on"; however, after the interview he decided that Tom seemed sincere and that furthermore "some of the details in Tom's story could not be found in any of the superficial UFO lore. I finally had to conclude Tom was on the level.[15]"

Keel was so convinced of Monteleone's veracity that he included his tale in an article ("The Time Cycle Factor") that appeared the March 1969 issue of *Flying Saucer Review*, his 1970 book *UFOs Operation Trojan Horse*, another article ("A Question of Responsibility") in the June 1971 issue of *Flying Saucers*, and, of course, in the *Mothman Prophecies* (1975).

You've probably already guessed the punch line.

Thomas J. Monteleone revealed the details of his

hoax in the "Last Word" column of the May 1979 edition of *Omni* magazine. The article, entitled "The Gullibility Factor," detailed how he called in to WWDC's Comment call-in show as a "harmless prank." Worse still, he noted how he added details to Derenberger's account and then deliberately contradicted the West Virginian's tale, only to have Derenberger backtrack and then adapt his story to agree with Monteleone's version!

This obviously casts further doubts on Derenberger's original story. Or at the very least, the stories he came up with afterward.

As his fame in UFO circles grew, Monteleone bragged that he would add something to the story each time.

What convinced Keel of his veracity was the novel inclusion of an old black Buick, of which Monteleone claimed, "It still had that 'new car smell' and the engine was ticking along like a Switch watch[16]." This allegedly prompted Keel to jump out of his chair, exclaiming, "That clinches it! You have just revealed to me important information that is not available to the public. There is no possible way you could have known about this unless it really happened to you[17]."

No possible way? Monteleone admits that he was aware of the Men in Black conspiracy, or the Silence group, as it's called, which was why he mentioned the old car that was remarkably new-looking, something MIBs were said to drive. This information wasn't well known outside UFO circles, but Monteleone notes that he "knew the lore[18]."

In fact, during his original taped interview with Harold Salkin and Derenberger, Monteleone realized at one point that they were conducting the interview in front of his bookshelf, which contained row upon row of sci-fi books, as well as books by Charles Fort and flying saucer books by Frank Edwards, J. Allen Hynek, Donald Keyhoe and perhaps even George Adamski. (Salkin apparently never noticed the contradiction.) He also recalls that when Salkin asked him to describe Lanulos in detail that he would just "conjure up some old *Galaxy* or *Planet Stories* cover and roll on[19]."

In any case, Keel was, initially, a great deal more shrewd. Monteleone himself noted that he thought the Keel suspected he was a fraud and that he had to think quickly on his feet. In fact, Keel reportedly told Monteleone that until his chance invocation of the Men in Black detail, he'd been convinced that the whole affair was just a "college prank" and that he'd supposed he was coming to expose Monteleone as a hoaxer[20]. (So close!)

Furthermore, Keel informed Derenberger, who was also present for the interview and I am sure did not like this one little bit, that he'd never really believed his tale; however. Keel assured him that "this young man has come up with enough facts to back it up. I'm forced to accept that it's true[21]."

Keel wasn't the only one taken in by Monteleone's hoax. Timothy Green Beckley, aka Mr. UFO, reportedly interviewed him before Keel did. Writing in his March 1970 "On the Trail of Flying Saucers" column, Beckley wrote, "Talking with Mr. Monteleone on several different occasions, including a two and a half hour TV special on Norman Ross's Comment (Channel 14 in Washington), we are convinced that Tom's experience, exactly as related took place[22]."

Well, after his confession in the May 1979 *Omni* article, Monteleone was featured an article in the November 1980 issue of *Fate* magazine. "Anatomy of a Hoax" by Karl T. Pflock made special note of Keel's credulity in the whole affair. According to Pflock, the editor nixed his original title, "Keel-Hauled by a Flying Saucer[23]." Keel responded by sending out a one-page statement entitled, "The Fickle Finger of Fate," which was discussed in the October 25, 1980 issue of Jim Moseley's *Saucer Smear* newsletter. Keel's response was predictable: he intended to sue and he never believed Monteleone's story in the first place. Curiously, he nonetheless claimed that "Monteleone still sticks to his story privately, and is denying it now just to get in good with the science fiction crowd[24]."

That's partly true. Monteleone did note concerns about his connection to UFO lore hurting his future sci-fi career when he recounted the tale in his "M.A.F.I.A" column for *Cemetery Dance* magazine in 2003[25].

By Saucer Logic, we would conclude that Monteleone is covering up the truth of a real alien contact for the sake of his career. By real logic, we would note that he said it was a hoax because it wasn't true. It was a prank that went too far, and one that associated him with a subject that could spell death for his intended writing career in those days. And maybe he'd started to believe his own press a bit too much.

Just after he began his published writing career in 1973, Monteleone co-wrote a play with Grant Carrington called "U.F.O!" The play was performed once on March 11, 1977 by the Sandy Springs Theater Group, Inc. (MD), two years before his *Omni* confession.

Carrington's description of the play reads:

> "As a prank, Vincent, a college senior, calls in to a radio talk show to verify the guest's visit to another world via UFO. Vincent is soon besieged by UFO "investigators," since (1) very few people have visited the same world as other UFO abductees and (2) he's a "University Graduate" instead of the usual handymen, etc. Vincent is asked to be the featured guest at a UFO convention and goes although his best friend and his girl friend [sic] are beginning to grow distant as Vincent himself begins to believe in his own prank. At the convention, during his

speech, he realizes what he's beginning to lose and denies his visit, although the UFOlogists don't want to believe it.[26]"

In his essay, "Keep Watching the Skies – Part 3", for *Cemetery Dance* #45 (2003), Monteleone himself has this to say about "U.F.O!":

"It's a funny play and the main character a college student, ends up wondering if all the things he made up actually happened, and the aliens have given him "screened memories" to mask his memories of the events – which I do have to tell you had cross my mind (albeit fleetingly) in our on [sic] time-space continuum[27]."

So maybe he did go down the rabbit hole a bit.

After the smoke of his admitted hoax cleared, "U.F.O!" made an encore performance during the summer of 1982 as the very first production of the first year of the Baltimore Playwrights Festival by the Fells Point Theatre. Interestingly enough, there is a character in the play named "Captain Leek," whom Monteleone identifies as "Jonathan Leek." Leek, as he notes, is simply Keel spelled backwards[28]. So even before his full confession, Monteleone was calling Keel out for his credulity.

When Mark Opsasnick interviewed Keel by phone in June 1991, Keel once again claimed that he'd known all along Monteleone was a fraud. There's certainly evidence to suggest that Keel entertained a few doubts about Monteleone because he definitely had some concerning Derenberger's tale! You see, although he'd assured Derenberger that Monteleone's story verified his own, when Keel wrote the Foreword on October 12, 1968 to the West Virginian contactee's 1971 book, *Visitors from Lanulos*, Keel took pains to make his skepticism evident:

> "I cannot endorse his story but I do feel I know the man well enough to give him a character reference. The important thing is that he seems to be telling the truth as he knows it. He sincerely believes that these things happened to him. And he is willing to expose himself to ridicule and condemnation in order to make himself heard… I'm not asking you to believe any of it. But I am asking you to listen to what he has to say."

In the *Mothman Prophecies*, he states that

> "Woodrow Derenberger's story troubled me from the outset, and for many reasons. It did not fit the mold of the usual UFO contact tale… They defied easy

classification and would not fit into any of the pigeonholes I had constructed. Either he was the world's most convincing liar, and had somehow trained his wife, children, and friends to back up his lies, or he had had a very special set of experiences beyond the limits of ufology[29]."

Also very after the fact, Keel wrote in 2002:

"As for Indrid Cold, I never talked to him on the telephone. I always thought Woodrow Derenberger probably made him up[30]."

So maybe he did have suspicions about the Lanulosian tales, but I don't think he was certain they were false. I say this because it's fair to ask, as Mike Opsasnick did when he questioned Keel on the matter, why Keel included material from Derenberger and Monteleone in the *Mothman Prophecies* as matters of fact. For the record, Keel dissembled when confronted, claiming that the lawyers wouldn't let him call anyone a fraud and that his statement in which he concludes Monteleone is on the level was in a chapter on hoaxes.

Of course, nothing forced him to include the false material in the first place... unless he was simply unaware it was, in fact, false. Both Monteleone and Derenberger's claims (by association) turned out to be hoaxes, but that's not how Keel wrote them in the

Mothman Prophecies' chapter entitled "Sideways in Time."

Speaking of time, in the first chapter of the 1996 IllumiNet Press edition of John Keel's *Operation: Trojan Horse* he calls Monteleone an "outright liar," (Where were the lawyers on that one?) and takes great pains to point out that the sci-fi author made up the contactee claim, but neither the original 1970 edition of the book nor even the 1973 Abacus edition of the book suggests anything of the sort! Like the 1969 "Time Cycle Factor" article, the 1973 edition relates Monteleone's Vadig story as a basis for Keel's assertion that "Part of the answer to flying saucers may lie not in the stars but in the clock ticking on your mantelpiece." Incidentally, the 1996 edition of *Operation: Trojan Horse* tries to keep the point about time while admitting that the story the point is based on is false. If Keel were alive today, I would remind him that truth nor credibility can be supported on a foundation of lies. Based on this, I believe he chose to give the Lanulosian tales the benefit of the doubt because they did, in fact, fit into the pigeonholes he had constructed, or at least a particular theory he favored.

Opsasnick notes that the 1991 IllumiNet Press edition of the *Mothman Prophecies* included a brand-new Afterword, penned on July 10, 1991, only a month after his phone interview with a blustering Keel. In this new material, Keel claims that he'd written to Long John Nebel explaining that he regarding Monteleone's tale as "a hilarious put-on and that all contactee stories were highly suspect, to put it kindly." Allegedly, Nebel read his letter on the air before introducing a flustered Monteleone on his all-night talk show in 1969[31]. In any case, Keel laments that Monteleone's "tale of bug-eyed men, rides in flying saucers, and visits to nonexistent planets have now become part of the lore despite my subtle inclusion of [Monteleone] in this book with the assorted foreign fakers. Some people just want to believe that there are nude space people out there somewhere[32]."

Indeed, as Keel himself noted in "A Question of Responsibility" (*Flying Saucers*, June 1971), one of the things that makes the UFO enigma so difficult to solve are those who muddy the waters "by accepting unverified nonsense as fact when it fell into the pattern of their beliefs." Credulity coupled with confirmation bias.

With this cautionary tale in hand, let's continue our exploration of the fascinating world of the saucerians.

***

Notes

1. Randle, Kevin. "An Editorial Comment." (June 22, 2007), Web: http://kevinrandle.blogspot.com/2007/06/editorial-comment.html. Retrieved May 18, 2016.

2. Derenberger, Woodrow W. "I Met a Man From Another World!" *Probe* 5, 1 (September 1968), pp. 8-11.

3. Don't get me started on how ironic it is that a magazine called *Probe* would do a story on alien abduction!

4. Keel, John A. *The Mothman Prophecies*. Tor edition (2001), p. 113.

5. Barker, Gray. "The Greatest Saucer Story Ever Told." *Gray Barker's Book of Adamski*. New Saucerian Press (2014), p.20. Originally printed by Saucerian Press (1967).

6. Robinson, Bob. "Skeptical Believer: Saucers Chronicled." *Spokane Daily Chronicle* (3 July 1979), p. 2.

7. Murphy, Jody. "Alien claims took toll on Derenbergers." *Parkersburg News & Sentinel*. June 11, 2011.

8. Derenberger, *Ibid*.

9. Murphy, *Ibid*.

10. Keel, John. The Complete Guide to Mysterious Creatures. Tor (2002), p. 197.

11. Murphy, *Ibid*.

12. *Mothman Prophecies*, p. 151.

13. Keel relates this tale of woe in both the introduction to Derenberger's *Visitors from Lanulos* and in Keel's own *The Complete Guide to Mysterious Beings* (p.197), though he only mentions Barkers part in the incident in the latter work.

14. "Derenberger Contact Claims." Clark, Jerome. *High Strangeness: Ufos from 1960 Through 1979 (UFO Encyclopedia, Vol. 3).* Omnigraphics Inc. (1993), pp. 153.

15. *Mothman Prophecies*, p. 196.

16. Pflock, Karl T. "Anatomy of a Hoax." Fate. Vol, 33. No. 11. Issue 368 (November 1980), p.46.

17. Monteleone, Thomas F. *Mother and Fathers Italian Association.* Borderlands Press (March 2003). Monteleone's confession was published in his Mother And Fathers Italian Association column in Cemetery Dance magazine in 2003. It originally appeared in three parts in three separate issues, and was eventually collected into this omnibus volume that won a 2003 Bram Stoker Award for non-fiction. His confessions comprises the last three chapters.

18. Opsasnick, Mark. "The Monteleone Contactee Case and the Route 40 Abduction Corridor." Strange magazine No. 15 (Spring 1995), p. 20.

19. Monteleone, *Ibid.*

20. Pflock, *Ibid.*

21. Beckley, Timothy Green. "On the Trail of Flying Saucers." *Flying Saucers: Mysteries of the Space Age.* No. 68 (March 1970). Beckley column picked up where Gray Barker's "Chasing the Flying Saucers" column left off when the latter quit writing for Ray Palmer's magazine.

22. Moseley, p. 273.

23. Moseley, James. "The Fickle Finger of Fate." *Saucer Rear* 27, No. 10 (October 25, 1980), p.3. Moseley's newsletter would eventually be called Saucer Smear, but at the time of the writing of this issue, he was still trying out names. This isn't one of the better ones.

24. Pflock, *Ibid*, p. 47.

25. Monteleone, *Ibid.*

26. http://www.grantcarrington.freeyellow.com/TimesFool/ufo.htm

27. Monteleone, *Ibid.*

28. When the 2002 *Mothman Prophecies* movie came out, the screenwriters used the same trick with a character named Alexander Leek.

29. Keel, John A. *Mothman Prophecies.* Tor (2002), p. 113.

30. Keel, John A. "Mothman Again," *Fate* (Vol. 55, No. 3, (April 2002), p. 6.

31. I haven't been able to corroborate this claim. Yet. Monteleone does confirm that Nebel didn't believe him, but he doesn't mention Keel's letter. As of the writing of this book, Monteleone hasn't responded to my query on the subject.

32. Keel, John A. *Mothman Prophecies*. Illuminet Press (1991), pp. 270-271. The Afterword these quotes are taken from only exists in this specific edition. No prior edition contained an Afterword and the 2002 Tor edition contains a completely different Afterword that doesn't mention Monteleone at all.

9 Saucerian Psychology

How To Foil An Alien Holocaust

Andy Sinatra, also known as the "Mystic Barber" or the "Cosmic Barber," was a contactee who believed he was a Martian stranded on Earth. He told Long John Nebel that he could always tell when another contactee was in his barber's chair because they cast no reflection in the mirror[1]. He claimed that flying saucers ran on solar power and could heal themselves.

"It is a very complicated process," he told Newspaper Enterprises Association's reporter Tom Tiede[2].

Apparently, saucers originated not from space but from inside the Earth where a group of aliens had taken refuge after their planet, Nova, exploded. He'd been to Venus, Mars[3], Uranus, Saturn, the Moon and the center of the Earth itself, but not in a saucer. Rather he uses astral projection to send his spirit to other planets and times, which he assures us is "a very complicated process."

He claimed that he could make such far out journeys by use of some special head gear that "looked suspiciously like old coat hangers covered in tin foil[4]," but which Sinatra claimed were so powerful that it caused an earthquake or tidal wave whenever he used the apparatus. In addition to giving Andy and his wife, Giovannina, joyrides and creating natural disasters as a by-product, the "psychic machines" they wore on their heads allegedly kept evil Space People who were still looking for the Novan refugees from reading their thoughts[5].

"It is a very complicated process," he assures us[6].

It must be complicated because if left to what we know of living conditions on other bodies in our solar system, not to mention the center of the Earth, we would have to dismiss such claims... unless we're going with the equally unverifiable claim that the versions of Mars, the Moon, Venus, etc., that these folk are visiting exist on a different dimensional plane and can't be seen by normal folk... especially not skeptics, right?

Sinatra's headgear eventually got more and more elaborate, until it looked like a "ridiculous metal beanie topped with what looked like a small Bazooka tube[7]." On February 4, 1962, armed with this apparatus and accompanied by an army of invisible Martians, Andy Sinatra single-handedly saved the world from "terrible destructive forces" which were, at the very least, intent on toppling the United Nations building in Manhattan if the world did not unite by the deadline given ninety days prior. Nothing happened, which shouldn't have been surprising given his previous failed prediction that the world would end during the week of May 10, 1960, but as Jim Moseley observes, tongue firmly in cheek:

> "Obviously Andy's mumbo-jumbo worked. The UN complex still stands today...[8]"

The Cosmic Barber is not the only one for whom alien contact is apparently all in one's head. Invisible aliens aren't uncommon in contactee circles, which is annoying because we can't independently verify them. It's one thing to say that the saucers are invisible via cloaking technology or translucent building materials or what-have-you, but this is way past nonsense like Wonder Woman and her invisible jet. It's even beyond the camouflage tech of a Predator-type alien (Best. Schwarzenegger. Movie. Ever.), because they aren't cloaked to everyone; only the contactee can see them!

Which brings us back to Derenberger. We must remind you that Derenberger's second encounter with Indrid Cold was more of a trance. The very nature of Derenberger's contacts with Cold led one of the investigators from the National Investigations Committee on Aerial Phenomenon (NICAP) to write that, while Derenberger's story couldn't be written off as a hoax or a fraud, "The question of whether Derenberger experienced an hallucination (possibly in conjunction with an epileptic seizure) cannot be ruled out[9]."

In case you're wondering, Derenberger was examined by a local psychiatrist, Dr. Alan Roberts[10], at St. Joseph's Hospital (Parkersburg, WV) in December 1966, at the urging of Kevin Dee and the NICAP Pittsburgh subcommittee. Derenberger was given a clean bill of mental health; however, as luck would have it, this particular shrink ended up becoming a contactee, too, leaving it rather doubtful that his assessment of Derenberger was altogether unbiased.

To be fair, at this point we have to have ask: what of other psychiatric evaluations of these contactees and abductees?

The Trouble With Hypnosis

In the July 24, 1992 edition of the *Harvard University Gazette*, alien abduction psychiatrist (yes, that's a real thing apparently) Dr. John E. Mack said that of the 60 cases he had worked on at the time, after a battery of psychological tests, "'no psychiatric or psychosocial explanation for these reports is evident. These people are not mentally ill.' Mack stated that what struck him about abductees was their "ordinariness." He concluded that "The majority of abductees do not appear to be deluded, confabulating, lying, self-dramatizing, or suffering from a clear mental illness[11]."

Apparently, his colleagues did not agree with his assessment of the data. In May 1994, the Dean of the Harvard School of Medicine appointed an investigative committee in which "Members were asked to examine whether Dr. Mack was conducting his research in accordance with Harvard's standards of scholarly investigation and whether he was exploiting his patients or subjecting them to harm." According to a February 9, 1995 letter[12] from Daniel Sheehan, Mack's attorney, the committee's Draft Report found "that it is professionally irresponsible for any academic, scholar or practicing psychiatrist to give any credence whatsoever to any personal report of a direct personal contact between a human being and an Extraterrestrial Being until after the person...has been subjected to every possible available battery of standard psychological tests which might conceivably explain the report as the product of some known form of clinical psychosis....To communicate, in any way whatsoever, to a person who has reported a 'close encounter' with an Extraterrestrial life form that this experience might well have been real...is professionally irresponsible."

This marked the first time a tenured professor was subjected to such an investigation at Harvard[13]. As a result, some folks, including Mack's Boston lawyer, Roderick MacLeish, saw it less as peer review than an attack on academic freedom.

In Harvard's defense, Mack was using hypnosis as a research tool. Oh, and there was also the fact that the April 25, 1994 issue of *Time* magazine had apparently brought the matter to their attention to begin with in conjunction with publication of Mack's book, *Abduction: Human Encounters with Aliens*. You see, that issue carried an article called, "The Man from Outer Space[14]," with the teaser line, "Harvard psychiatrist John Mack claims that tales of UFO abductions are real. But experts and former patients say his research is shoddy."

The article included the account of Donna Bassett, a 37-year old Boston-based writer and researcher, who decided to go undercover "after hearing complaints that he was 'strip mining' the stories of emotionally distraught people and failing to help them with follow-up therapy."

According to Bassett, she got into Mack's program and rather imaginatively faked her way through three hypnotic-regression sessions, even relating an encounter aboard a spaceship during the Cuban Missile Crisis with John F. Kennedy and a sobbing Nikita Khrushchev, the latter of whom Bassett consoled.

> "'I sat in his lap, and I put my arms around his neck, and I told him it would be O.K.' Hearing her tale, Mack became so excited that he leaned on the bed too heavily, and it collapsed[15]."

She also said that she was provided with UFO literature to read prior to her sessions, something that medical hypnotists and anyone with any amount of sense would realize would influence hypnotic revelations. Mack counter-charged that he'd met Bassett at a UFO conference and that he sent her the literature prior to her even becoming a patient of his. He also noted that despite her claim that he was "ecstatic" over her contactee account, that he did not include it in his book, so... maybe he wasn't as credulous as she supposed[16].

Then again, on NOVA's "Kidnapped by UFOs?", which aired on February 27, 1996, Mack said of Bassett:

"I mean, I worked with Donna in good faith and she claims she was all a hoax. And people I know in the experienced community think that she did not hoax, that she's an experiencer who never came to terms with her experience[17]."

He seemed to be of two minds on the subject.

In the end, Mack was censured in the committee's report for what they believed were methodological errors, but the Dean took no action on it; instead, they restored his good standing and reaffirmed his academic freedom. Since none of the committee members will comment and there is a dearth of paperwork associated with the 14-month investigation that took place in at least 30 closed door sessions, we can only speculate as to whether the outcome was determined by their findings or by the media campaign being waged against them by Mack's counsel. And also a large financial donation from a Mack supporter. If I were being generous, I'd suggest that there's a little bit of truth to both sides of that equation. Alas! I'm a cynic, especially when lawyers get involved.

Another fellow who is well-known for his psychiatric opinions about abductees is Wheeling, WV native Budd Hopkins. Hopkins was dubbed the "father of the abduction movement," mostly for popularizing the idea of alien abductions as genetic experiments through his 1987 book, *Intruders: The Incredible Visitations at Copley Woods*. Hopkins was trained as an artist, not a psychiatrist (though he has partnered in research with real psychiatrists and psychologists like Dr. John Mack, Dr. Aphrodite Clamar, and Dr. Elizabeth Slater); apparently, the popularity of his books and ideas have caused folks to overlook that little fact.

Once again, the super-duper-reliable method of hypnotism was used. On NOVA's "Kidnapped by UFOs?", psychologist Elizabeth Loftus identified "subtle but powerful suggestive cues" as Budd Hopkins worked with two children during a taped hypnosis session aired on the show[18]. Many experts concur that hypnosis makes someone suggestible. For example, Fred Frankel, at the time a Harvard Medical School professor and psychiatrist-in-chief at Boston's Beth Israel hospital, stated:

> "Hypnosis helps you regain memories that you would not have otherwise recalled... But some will be true, and some will be false. The expectation of the hypnotist and the expectation of the person who is going to be hypnotized can influence the result.[19]"

Dr. Jacques Vallee believes that hypnosis can create "abductees":

> "I think that the way abductions are being handled is wrong. It's not only wrong scientifically, it's wrong morally and ethically. I've

been telling people, don't let anyone hypnotize you if you've seen a strange light in the sky. I think a lot of those people prominent in the press and in the National Enquirer and in the talk shows and so on are creating abductees under hypnosis. They are hypnotizing everybody who's ever had a strange experience and telling them they are abductees by suggestion. And they are doing that in good faith. They don't realize what they are doing. But to my way of thinking, that's unethical.[20]"

During the aforementioned NOVA episode, Loftus also cautioned that someone convinced of a false memory can react emotionally to it and elaborate on the story as if it were real[21].

These cautions regarding hypnosis contrast sharply with the prevailing attitudes of many in the UFO community on the subject. For example, Jim and Coral Lorenzen's Aerial Phenomena Research Organization (APRO) found it revealing "that Woodrow Derenberger refused to submit to hypnotic questioning, saying that Air Force representatives advised him not to[22]."

Psychologist Richard Ofshe, an expert on hypnotism, adds:

"If you convince someone they've been brutalized and raped, and you encourage them to fully experience the emotions appropriate for this event - and the event never happened - you've led them through an experience of pain that is utterly gratuitous[23]."

Other factors, such as sensory deprivation, can increase suggestibility.

Anyway, based on the research of his aforementioned partners (who do not necessarily agree with his conclusions), interviews and group therapy sessions with abductees, Hopkins likens abductees to rape victims[24]. He concluded, based on their oft-times nightmarish experiences, that either the aliens "have not grasped the psychological toll they are taking in these abductions and genetic experiments because they really do not understand human psychology, or they must be viewed as a callous, indifferent, amoral race bent solely upon gratifying its own scientific needs at whatever the cost to us, the victims[25]." At some point, he began to be inclined to dismiss his clients' conscious memory of actual abuse for more alien explanations;[26] basically, he believes that memories of abuse by aliens are repressed with false memories of abuse by humans, which is nothing more than self-serving, potentially harmful, one-size-fits-all Saucer Logic as far as I'm concerned.

Irregardless of the subjective realities of hypnosis-drawn memories, sleep paralysis has been suggested as a probable explanation for alleged alien abductions. Sleep paralysis is a condition in which an individual, a transitional state between wakefulness and sleep, temporarily experiences an inability to move, speak, or react. It can be a terrifying experience. The obvious helplessness is sometimes accompanied by hallucinations of intruders in the room or outside the window or door. In some cases, the victim feels chest pressure or the feeling of being strangled or prodded. Combined with hypnosis-drawn memories and the cultural ubiquity of extraterrestrial motifs, it's no wonder some of these poor folks think they're being abducted by aliens!

Beyond MKUltra

CIA mind control projects. It sounds like something out of a movie In fact, if you've seen films like the Jason Bourne series, based on the novels of Robert Ludlum, you have some idea of what the CIA's very real MKUltra project was about.

Just to make sure everyone is on the same page, you should know that MKUltra was a secret program of human experiments, much of which was very illegal in the fact that they were often conducted without the subject's knowledge or permission. This included experiments with LSD and other drugs, hypnosis, sensory deprivation, isolation, psychological torture, and even verbal and sexual abuse. The program was vast, consisted of 149 subprojects in the United

States and Canada conducted from 1953 to 1973. Although 80 institutions (including universities, pharmaceutical companies, hospitals, prisons, and mental institutions) and 185 individual researchers participated in MKUltra research, many were unaware that they were working for the CIA because the project was funded indirectly.

While MKUltra sounds like a good conspiracy theory, it has been confirmed a cache of 20,000 documents relating to project obtained through the Freedom of Information Act in 1977 and a release of surviving declassified information regarding the project in July 2001. This was despite the fact that CIA Director Richard Helms ordered all MKUltra files destroyed in 1973. Obviously, they missed a few.

It should come as little surprise that MKUltra was born out of the mind control projects of Nazi scientists obtained through Operation Paperclip.

What does this have to do with Ufology? Well, recall that when the 1953 CIA-sponsored Robertson Panel identified private UFO groups as a potential threat, they were worried that "related dangers might well exist resulting from… Subjectivity of public to mass hysteria and greater vulnerability to possible enemy psychological warfare." You tend to be worried about the enemy using the things you yourself are doing.

Given the fact that CIA mind control experiments

seemed to have coincided with the Robertson Panel warning about the potential dangers of private UFO groups, this opens up the question of whether Albert K. Bender was subjected to hallucinogenic drugs or hypnosis against his knowledge. It's inarguably the stuff of conspiracy theories, but with the confirmed existence of diabolical CIA mind control programs, it becomes an intriguing possibility.

One also wonders if MILABs are a clue that the CIA is more involved in the UFO phenomenon that one at first suspects. The term MILAB is a neologism for "MILitary Abduction." Basically, depending upon your point of view, these are military operations performed to convince the targets that they are being abducted by extraterrestrials or military abductions with the aid of aliens and their alien abduction technology. The latter is conspiracy fodder. It seems the government is always selling out its people in exchange for extraterrestrial technology. What's interesting is the little reported fact that sometimes abductees report that there are humans working alongside their alien captors. Frankly, this make the former concept of MILABs more attractive as a possibility, in that it makes me wonder if MKUltra-type methods aren't being used to stage abductions as part of some CIA psychological experiment. It might seem too elaborate to be true at first glance but when you consider the lengths the government went through to convince Paul Bennewitz of an alien conspiracy, including feeding him false extraterrestrial signals and staging crash remnants, a little LSD and a dash of hypnosis seems like a short cut in comparison!

Something more in line with the Robertson Panel's cautions is Jacques Vallee's warnings about human-made UFO conspiracies, given during a 1995 Conspire.com interview:

"'I was investigating some cases that were physically real,' he says, 'but they were hoaxes--yet not hoaxes on the part of the witnesses.' ...In 1980, a strange object purportedly 'crashed' in England's Rendlesham Forest, a few miles away from an American Air Force Base. Dozens of military personnel were dispatched into the forest, without weapons, before the supposed crash of a luminous object. After the incident conflicting stories leaked to the press and to civilian investigators, some of the leaks apparently originating from the front office of the military base. Vallee's conclusion--controversial among UFO believers who insist that aliens touched down in Rendlesham Forest--is that 'the event had all the earmarks of being staged for the benefit of the witnesses, perhaps so that their psychological reactions could be studied[27].'

One is reminded of a rather bizarre FEMA exercise involving a "zombie UFO crash" scenario which was conducted in the town of Moscow, Idaho on April 27, 2013. Shortly after Nevada gubernatorial candidate David Lory VanDerBeek wrote an article questioning whether the government really thought UFOs and zombies were a real and imminent threat, FEMA censored the announcement of the drill from its site.

While the training exercise was billed as a "whimsical" way to carry out very real mass casualty and rope rescue drills, the fact that it wasn't the first time the authorities had played to a zombie apocalypse as a measure of disaster preparedness fed a lot of internet-based fearmongering of both the zombie apocalypse and UFO impending disclosure conspiracy varieties. Two birds with the same stone.

For the record, the Center for Disease Control (CDC) printed zombie survival materials in 2011 under the rationalization that "If you are generally well equipped to deal with a zombie apocalypse you will be prepared for a hurricane, pandemic, earthquake, or terrorist attack." A year later (September 2012), the Department of Homeland Security (DHS) chimed in that zombie apocalypse preparedness was equivalent to more mundane disaster preparedness. Putting its money where its mouth is, the DHS sponsored a drill the very next month on an island off the coast of San Diego involving US Marines and

Navy special forces centered on the premise of a zombie invasion. That particular exercise was also attended by no less than former CIA Director Michael Hayden, making one wonder whether, just maybe, these UFO and zombie scenarios aren't part of some CIA psychological experiment aimed at the public. To what purpose? You ask. Well, if I had to lay money on it, I'd wager that it all goes back to the potential danger of mass panic revealed in Orson Welles' 1938 radio broadcast of *The War of the Worlds*. At the very least, these scenarios serve to gauge the population's reaction to such scenarios and, perhaps to inoculate us against a full-fledged panic if a foreign enemy started a propaganda war to cause mayhem in advance of an attack. Food for thought.

Cinema Strikes Back

Speaking of the influence of the media, Ufologist and cryptozoologist Nick Redfern has noted that Indrid Cold, Woodrow Derenberger's "Grinning Man," bears an uncanny resemblance to a character in ABC's sci-fi series, *The Invaders*. The series starred Roy Thinnes as David Vincent, an architect who accidentally learns of a secret alien invasion already underway, forcing him to travel from place to place in order to foil the aliens' plots and keep the show interesting. In an episode entitled "Panic[28]," which originally aired on April 11, 1967, an alien going by the name of Nick Baxter (played by guest star Robert Walker Jr., better known to Trekkies as Charlie X from *Star Trek: The Original Series*[29]) causes death and, yes, panic as he travels through rural West Virginia. The human-looking alien puts up a front of being friendly and helpful, but carries a virus that literally freezes and kills anyone Baxter touches.

Hmm... Could there be a connection? It wouldn't be the first time a contactee's experiences mirrored a pop culture reference.

We've already mentioned the fact that many witnesses described disc, saucer or hubcap shaped UFOs in the wake of the 1947 Kenneth Arnold sighting, based on newspaper reports, even though Kenneth Arnold's UFOs weren't actually saucer-shaped. We also mentioned that, prior to the release of Steven Spielberg's *Close Encounters of the Third Kind* (1977), there were no records of Greys with long, thin necks in UFO literature, but they started popping up afterwards. It is unlikely that aliens would change their own shape or the shape of their craft to conform to our expectations.

The case of Barney and Betty Hill provides another instance where cultural expectations played a role. The "Hill Abduction" or the "Zeta Reticula Incident" is significant because it is considered to be the first classic alien abduction case. Their story was popularized in a 1966 book called *The Interrupted Journey* and in a 1975 television movie called *The UFO Incident*, starring James Earl Jones and Estelle Parsons.

The event itself was alleged to take place on the night of September 19, 1961 and the morning after, while the Hills were driving back from a vacation in Montreal and Niagara Falls to their home in Lancaster, New Hampshire. They sighted a UFO through binoculars at a scenic picnic area near Twin Mountain. As they continued their journey, they continued to see the craft, until it halted their progress approximately one mile south of Indian Head. Barney stepped out of the car with his pistol in his pocket. Using the binoculars, Barney allegedly spotted 8 to 11 humanoid figures clad in glossy black hats and uniforms through the craft's windows, looking back at him. One spoke to Barney telepathically (Tell me you saw *that* coming) to "stay where you are and keep looking." Barney ran back to the car in a panic and drove off. The saucer gave chase. The couple lost consciousness after experiencing a series of rhythmic buzzing and beeping sounds. When they regained consciousness, they'd driven 35 miles with no recollection.

Betty reported the UFO incident to officials at Pease Air Force Base on September 21, 1961. Major Paul W. Henderson conducted a telephone interview the next day. His September 26th report concluded that the couple had likely misidentified Jupiter.

After reading one of his UFO books, *The Flying Saucer Conspiracy*, Betty wrote to Major Donald Keyhoe who was then the head of the civilian UFO investigation group called NICAP. A NICAP interview conducted on October 21, 1961, revealed that Barney had developed a "mental block," but he described the craft's occupants as "somehow not human."

In November, Betty began writing down the details of strange dreams she'd been having since about ten days after the UFO incident. In one dream, men surrounded their car at a roadblock. After briefly losing consciousness, she finds that they were being forced to walk in a forest by two men, who were described as being about five feet to five feet four inches tall and wore matching blue uniforms, with caps similar to those worn by military cadets. She also said that they had greyish color skin, black hair, dark eyes, prominent noses and bluish lips. She and Barney, who appeared to be in a trance, were taken up the ramp of a flying saucer and herded off to separate examination rooms by their English-speaking captors. A subsequent NICAP interview confirmed that the couple were also "missing time," as they arrived at their destination at a much later time than they should have.

The Hills underwent hypnosis under Dr. Benjamin Simon, beginning in January 1964. Barney's version of the alleged abduction under hypnosis included a sperm sample and the dread anal probe (a feature of abductions that wouldn't become commonplace until Whitley Strieber burst upon the UFO scene with his alleged account of his own hypnosis-revealed abduction in his *New York Times* bestseller *Communion* (1987)). Barney Hill also mentioned that the aliens had "wraparound eyes."

Betty's sessions were more detailed. Intriguingly, the Jimmy Durante noses of her dream aliens were absent, replaced by nose-less aliens in hypnosis. After the sessions, Simon speculated that Barney's recollection of the UFO encounter was possibly a fantasy inspired by Betty's dreams.

The encounter might have faded were it not for a front page story in the October 25, 1965 issue of the *Boston Traveler*. The newspaper headline sported the very Halloweenish title, "UFO Chiller: Did THEY Seize Couple?" Apparently, reporter John H. Luttrell had received an audio recording of a lecture the Hills gave on November 3, 1963 to the Two State UFO Study Group, in Quincy Center, Massachusetts. UPI picked up the story the following day. After their story made international headlines, they were approached with a book deal.

Martin Kottmeyer has suggested that the wraparound eyes Barney Hill mentioned were borrowed from an *Outer Limits* episode called "The Bellero Shield," which aired on February 10, 1964. Barney Hill first described these wraparound eyes in a hypnosis session conducted on February 22, 1964. As supporting evidence for this theory, he notes that when Judith (played by Sally Kellerman) asks the "Bifrost alien" if he can read minds, it replies, "No, I cannot read your mind. I cannot even understand your language. I analyze your eyes. In all the universes, in all the unities beyond all the universes, all who have eyes have eyes that speak... I learn each word just before I speak it. Your eyes teach me." This is significant because in that same February 22nd session Barney Hill says, "Yes. They won't talk to me. Only the eyes are talking to me. I-I-I-I don't understand that. Oh-the eyes don't have a body. They're just eyes...[30]"

Kottmeyer has also noted that the Keyhoe book Betty Hill read just after the initial UFO sighting has tale of a person being dragged into a glowing UFO by four little men[31]. Furthermore, the Hill Abduction bears several points of similarity to the 1953 film *Invaders From Mars*, including Jimmy Durante noses, examination tables, needles, optical pacification techniques and even star maps[32].

The first time an alien abduction was featured in a science fiction work was way back in 1898. Garrett P. Serviss' science fiction serial *Edison's Conquest of Mars*, published in book form in 1947, was also the first such story to feature spacesuits, space battles, oxygen pills, asteroid mining and disintegrator rays. Serviss' story was a sequel to *Fighter from Mars*, an unauthorized serial of H.G. Wells' *War of the Worlds*. Likewise, the major points of the abduction narrative were already established in a 1930 Buck Rogers strip in which Martian "Tiger Men" capture a human female and examine her in their spaceship. She also sees the Earth from space during the journey, which act is described by abduction researchers as a theophany.

The concept of missing time and alien hybrids also preceded the advent of the abduction movement. For example, John Wyndham's 1957 *The Midwich Cuckoos*, later thrice made into a movie, *Village of the Damned* (1960 & 1995, respectively) and

Children of the Damned (1964), featured a plot in which every child-bearing woman in the fictional town of Midwich[33], Wilshire is impregnated by xenogenesis during a period of unnatural unconsciousness called "Dayout."

The Men in Black first described by Albert K. Bender may have also had their origin in cinema. Nick Redfern has suggested that their description was drawn from the 1949 Hammer Studios production *The Man in Black*, in which the narrator is a cloaked fellow in a black hat. A 1934 film called *Liliom* has also been suggested as an influence. The film contains some distinctly MIB-looking figures. Albert K Bender was a fan of Max Steiner, the "father of film music." In fact, he founded the Max Steiner Music Society in 1965. The music for *Liliom* was composed by Franz Waxman. Nick Redfern has pointed out that Waxman worked with Steiner but they did so post-1943, so the connection is admittedly vague. Of course, the MIB outfit is pretty generic and has been featured in everything from *The Shadow* to stock villains. Still, Bender was a noted horror and movie buff, so it's possible.

A Word on Mental Illness

There is a tendency in some Christian circles to overemphasize the Devil.

In *The Screwtape Letters*, CS Lewis noted:

> "There are two equal and opposite errors into which our race can fall

about the devils. One is to disbelieve in their existence. The other is to believe, and to feel an excessive and unhealthy interest in them. They themselves are equally pleased by both errors and hail a materialist or a magician with the same delight."

I am not denying that there is an occult aspect to some branches of Ufology (in fact, the very next chapter will examine them), but this does not mean that purely psychological explanations should be ruled out in many cases. In fact, I'm arguing that psychological causes should be considered before the supernatural is invoked.

If we insist that all contactee/abductee tales that aren't fabricated are the work of demonic forces, we are essentially saying that mental illnesses and psychosis are likewise demonic. I don't think we're quite that medieval in our comprehension of the physical world anymore. We might say, "God bless you!" when someone sneezes but we do so out of politeness and care rather than the fear that demons are flying out of the afflicted's nostrils, as we once did.

In the August 1977 issue of *Nucleus*, a publication of the UK-based Christian Medical Fellowship, Chris Cook[34] admonished his fellow Christians in psychiatry:

"We have an important

responsibility. We need to be informed of the findings and limits of psychiatric research, so that we can offer rational scientific explanations and treatments for psychiatric illness, where these exist"; however, he also noted that "if science does not have convincing answers, then we look elsewhere."

Since we would expect the greater number of answers to have natural causes, this approach would be the wisest.

His article concluded that "the relationship between these two concepts is complex"; however, they "are not simply alternative diagnoses to be offered when a person presents with deliberate self-harm or violent behavior."

Cook further notes:

> "Demon possession may be an aetiological factor in some cases of mental illness, but it may also be an aetiological factor in some non-psychiatric conditions, and in other cases it may be encountered in the absence of psychiatric or medical disorder. Furthermore, demon possession is essentially a spiritual problem, but mental illness is a multifactorial affair, in which

spiritual, social, psychological and physical factors may all play an aetiological role."

He cautioned that both psychiatric knowledge and spiritual discernment were necessary.

On a pragmatic level, Dr. Stephen Waterhouse has noted:

> "If prayer solves the problem, then it was probably not schizophrenia. If medicine helps alleviate the problem, it was not demon possession. Demons cannot be exorcised by phenothiazine, antidepressant drugs, or E.C.T.[35]"

Waterhouse also cites Dr. M. J. Sall, who wrote in the *Journal of Psychology & Theology*:

> "Hallucinations are cured by psychological treatment, while demon possession can be cured only by prayer and fasting as Christ indicated.[36]"

I would further caution that the same Jesus who has authority over devils also has authority over everything else. Meaning that even if you pray it away, it might not be the Lord casting out demons so much as the Great Physician curing someone.

I am reminded of one of my favorite stories in the Bible, the account of the man born blind in John chapter 9. It's an instructive tale because it happened because Jesus' disciples asked Him, "Rabbi, who sinned, this man or his parents, that he was born blind?"

> Jesus answered, "Neither this man nor his parents sinned, but that the works of God should be revealed in him."

In other words, He challenged them that it wasn't about the source so much as the Cure. As the parent of children with disabilities, I can tell you that I don't think Jesus was saying, "Nobody sinned. I made Him blind so I could cure him and you could all be impressed with Me and know that I'm the Son of God," although I certainly am impressed and all that. Rather Jesus was saying, "This guy who was born blind isn't being punished. He wasn't born as an object lesson for the consequences of sin. He was born blind for the same reason as everyone else: that the works of God should be manifest in Him." According to the Bible, people were created in the image of God. Our purpose, whether we choose to fulfill it or not, and even whether or not we suffer the effects of a fallen world more acutely than those around us, is to evidence the reality of God.

Treat the people around you accordingly.

***

Notes

1. How does he tell contactees from vampires??

2. Tiede, Tom. "UFO: Who's Kidding Whom? The Man Who Died Planet Hops." *Decatur Daily Review*. (December 7, 1966), p. 17.

3. Incidentally, according to the Mystic Barber of Brooklyn, Martians are four feet tall, are covered in white hair, and have reproductive organs in their heads.

4. Tiede, *Ibid.*

5. Moseley, James W., & Karl T. Pflock. *Shockingly Close to the Truth! Confessions of a Grave-Robbing Ufologist.* Prometheus Books (2002), p. 160.

6. Tiede, *Ibid.*

7. Moseley, *Ibid.*

8. *Ibid.*

9. "Derenberger Contact Claims." Clark, Jerome. *High Strangeness: Ufos from 1960 Through 1979 (UFO Encyclopedia, Vol. 3).* Omnigraphics Inc. (1993), pp. 154-55

10. Colvin, Andy. "Mothman: Angel of Conspiracy." *BeforeItsNews.com* (June 11, 2013), Web. Retrieved July 3, 2016.

11. Lord, Deane W. "John Mack on Abductions." Harvard University Gazette (July 24, 1992).

Web: http://www.textfiles.com/ufo/UFOBBS/2000/ 2726.ufo. Retrieved May 18, 2016.

12. Klass, Philip J. "Mack's Harvard Tenure Reportedly Threatened By Faculty Investigation." *The Skeptics UFO Newsletter. Volume 32.* CSICOP.org. March 1, 1995. http://www.csicop.org/specialarticles/show/klass_files_volume_32.

13. "No Censure for Professor Who Studies U.F.O.'s," *New York Times*, 4 August 1995, p. A15.

14. Willwerth, James. "The Man From Outer Space," *Time* 25 April 1994, pp. 74-75.

15. Ibid.

16. "Dr. John E. Mack's Response to Nova. Letter. (February 22, 1996). Web: http://www.beyondweird.com/ufos/John_Mack_Letter_To_Nova_February_1996.html. Retrieved May 18, 2016.

17. "Kidnapped by UFOs?" *PBS NOVA* Transcripts. February 27, 1996. Web: http://www.pbs.org/wgbh/nova/transcripts/2306tufos.html. Retrieved May 18, 2016.

18. Ibid.

19. Willwerth, *Ibid.*

20. *60GCAT.* "Heretic Among Heretics: Jacques Vallee Interview." Part 1. *Conspire.com.* [Undated, but evidently conducted prior to 2005] Web. Archived at https://web.archive.org/web/20031206075110/http://www.conspire.com/val.html.

21. *PBS NOVA, Ibid.*

22. "Man Claims Contact." *The A.P.R.O. Bulletin* (November-December 1966), p. 8.

23. Willwerth, *Ibid.*

24. Hopkins, Budd. "Ethical implications of the UFO abduction phenomenon." (September 1987). Web. http://www.bibliotecapleyades.net/vida_alien/alien_abductionabductees22.htm. Retrieved May 18, 2016.

25. *Ibid.*

26. Luckhurst, Roger. "The Science-fictionalization of Trauma: Remarks on Narratives of Alien Abduction". *Science Fiction Studies* 25.1 (1998): 29–52. Web. Retrieved May 18, 2016.

27. *60GCAT,* "Heretic Among Heretics: Jacques Vallee Interview." Part 1. *Conspire.com.* [Undated, but evidently conducted prior to 2005] Web. Archived at https://web.archive.org/web/2003121122342

4/http://www.conspire.com/val3.html.

28. "Panic." Season 1 Episode 14. *The Invaders* (Originally aired April 11, 1967) ABC.

29. "Charlie X." Season 1 Episode 7. *Star Trek: The Original Series*. (Originally aired September 15, 1966) NBC.

30. Kottmeyer, Martin. "The Eyes That Spoke." *CSICOP.org*. Web. Originally published in *Skeptical Briefs* Volume 4.3 (September 1994). Retrieved October 2, 2016.

31. Kottmeyer, Martin. "Gauche Encounters: Bad films and the UFO Mythos." *Talkingpix.co.uk*. Web. Retrieved October 2, 2016.

32. *Ibid.*

33. Yes, the fictional town of Midwich, West Virginia in my first novel, *Johnny Came Home*, is named after the town in Wyndam's novel.

34. Cook, Chris. "Demon Possession and Mental Illness" Nucleus (Autumn 1977), pp. 13-17.

35. Waterhouse, Stephen. *Strength For His People: A Ministry For Families of the Mentally Ill*. Westcliff Press (1994), p. 77.

36. *Ibid.*

10 It's All the Devil Anyway

Honestly, most Christians aren't all that concerned about lights or objects in the sky. We're perfectly willing to chalk those pesky UFOs to as-yet-unidentified terrestrial or atmospheric culprits, or even optical illusions. It's the contactee, abductee and Ancient Astronaut claims that bother us. In fact, it is these aspects of Ufology that cause us to consider whether the whole thing is a Satanic deception.

Among the first explanations proffered for the flying saucer phenomenon, well before any contactee or abductee accounts, were secret government or foreign aircraft, extraterrestrial craft, dero craft and what are now called ultraterrestrials. The latter two need clarification.

The Shaver Mystery and Saucers

We'll start with the dero craft, mostly because the idea predates the ultraterrestrial idea. One of the first saucerian theories was called the Shaver Mystery, which basically had it that the saucers were piloted by extraterrestrials in league with subterranean creatures called the abanondero, or dero (which stood for "detrimental robots"). The dero weren't really robots in the sense that we use the word now. They were evil creatures left behind by their creators, Atlans and Titans, who had lived underground in the great cavern cities of Lemuria until the radioactivity of our Sun forced them to leave. The sadistic dero used advanced technology left behind by their creators to send evil thoughts to humanity and to abduct us. Long before the Abductee movement which began in the 1960s, the original abductees could look forward to being tortured, raped, healed with miraculous machines so that they could be tortured and raped some more, and often eaten. The dero were H.G. Wells' Morlocks transplanted to a contemporary setting. They were demons in the flesh and they were opposed by a smaller group of abandoned creations called the tero.

The Shaver Mystery first appeared in the January 1944 issue of *Amazing Stories* in the form of a letter from Richard Shaver received by editor Ray Palmer in September 1943. In the letter, Shaver claimed to have discovered an ancient language called Mantong, which was the source of all other human languages and was "definite proof of the Atlantean legend." When Palmer received an overwhelmingly positive response in the form of hundreds of letters from *Amazing*'s readers, he wrote Shaver back, asking him how he'd stumbled upon Mantong, which prompted Shaver to write a 10,000-plus page alternate history of the Earth called, "A Warning to Future Man." Shaver told how in 1942 he'd begun hearing the voices of his co-workers coming from his welder. He also heard a disturbing torture session from subterranean dwellers. Later he claims he was kidnapped by the dero and held prisoner for almost a decade until the tero helped him to escape.

Palmer expanded the "Warning to Future Man" letter into a 31,000 page novella and renamed it "I

Remember Lemuria," which was published in the March 1945 issue of *Amazing Stories*. The response was overwhelming. The issue sold out and subscriptions skyrocketed. The Shaver Mystery series became immensely popular. For the next several years, every single issue contained at least one Shaver story, culminating in an all-Shaver issue in June 1947. Notoriously, the mythos Palmer and Shaver created together was presented as fact in an entertaining wrapper. Palmer regularly printed letters from folks who claimed to have real involvement with the fictional dero and who formed Shaver Mystery Clubs in several cities.

But were the dero real?

It's recognized now that Shaver suffered "from several of the classic symptoms of paranoid schizophrenia, and that many of the letters pouring into *Amazing* recounting personal experiences that backed up the author's stories patently came from the sorts of people who would otherwise spend their time claiming that they were being persecuted by invisible voices or their neighbor's dog[1]."

It's also noteworthy that Shaver's fantasies reflected a Christian worldview of angels and demons (though in numbers of the opposite proportions stated in Scripture) translated through a filter of mental illness and what Palmer called "extreme materialism[2,3]." Shaver's concrete worldview transformed hell into a place in subterranean caverns where one prayed for death as an escape rather than a punishment after death. By contrast, Palmer, a spiritualist, "believed in

God, an afterlife, a spiritual world, and paranormal powers[4]."

When Kenneth Arnold saw his "flying saucers" on June 24, 1947, Palmer took it as confirmation of the Shaver Mystery. In the October 1947 issue of *Amazing Stories*, Palmer declared that "A portion of the now world-famous Shaver Mystery has now been proved! On June 25th ...mysterious supersonic vessels, either space ships or ships from caves, were sighted in this country!" He went on to note that this confirmed Shaver's claim that "our earth is being visited regularly by ships from outer space."

Palmer had seemingly predicted the advent of flying saucers two months prior to Kenneth Arnold's sighting, when he wrote, just for fun, in the April 1947 issue:

> "Within a few years, we will be visited from outer space by a ship that will be seen all over the earth as it circles the planet, but such a ship as no one could have imagined even in our pages up to now."

After Ziff-Davis finally put a lid on the Shaver mystery, likely due to mounting objections from science fiction fans, Palmer set his sights on flying saucers. While still employed by Ziff-Davis, he began putting together a new magazine. *Fate* magazine debuted in March 1948, featuring a story from Kenneth Arnold himself. Palmer initially listed himself as editor as the pseudonymous Robert N. Webster, the same name he provided as a member of Albert K. Bender's International Flying Saucer Bureau's international council. Arnold's UFO account was listed under the title "I Did See the Flying Discs!" (although it was titled "The Truth About the Flying Saucers!" on the cover). The story was significant because now Palmer's magazines were suggesting an extraterrestrial origin for UFOs rather than the subterranean origin of the Shaver Mystery. *Fate* magazine became the flagship for the new growing UFO phenomenon.

Etheric Aeroforms

Another person who saw Kenneth Arnold's UFO report as proof of his theory was Meade Layne of the Borderland Sciences Research Foundation. Layne was also a member of the IFSB's international council.

Meade Layne's organization sent a "Statement of Importance" to the FBI on July 8, 1947, shortly after the Arnold sighting advocating the Etherian explanation to the UFO mystery. The document in the FBI's UFO vault files mentions the BSRA's *Round Robin* and *Flying Rolls* at the top. The document mentions a flying saucer account phoned in on October 9, 1946 by medium Dr. Mark Probert, reported in the October 1946 (Vol 2. No. 10) issue of *Round Robin*[5]. By a "curious coincidence," the next day this same psychic medium revealed through clairaudience that this UFO was a "kareeta," an extraterrestrial vessel. Layne admitted that this could be "an elaborate hoax by the communicating intelligences." You see, Layne was well aware that the "communicating intelligences" his mediums consorted with were perfectly capable of deception. Nevertheless, he reported in the next issue that, per Mark Probert:

"We understand it is the present intention of the Kareeta people to return in one year.[6]"

When the Arnold story broke, the BSRF, like Palmer, took it as confirmation of their psychics' claims. In the July/August issue of Round Robin, Layne mentions the Arnold sighting and connected it with the kareeta. At this point, his mediums, including Probert, "revealed" that the saucers were "etheric in nature, and they materialize spontaneously on entering the vibration rate of your world of dense matter. I think this is going to stir up a hell of a lot of trouble. The great trouble, of course, is with your scientists, they can't get into the right way of thinking about such problems[7]. "

The BSRA was the apparent source of one of the better-known hoaxes in Ufology: President Eisenhower's meeting with extraterrestrials at Muroc (later known as Edwards) Air Force Base. The source of the hoax is a letter dated April 16, 1954 to Meade Layne from BSRA member Gerald Light. Light claimed that on February 20th and 21st of 1954, he had been invited, along with Franklin Allen, Bishop (later Cardinal) Macintyre of Los Angeles, and President Truman's one-time financial adviser

Edwin Norse to Murdoc AFB, where they observed five different types of flying saucers being flown and examined by U.S. Air Force personnel "– with the assistance and permission of the Etherians!" That's right. The BSRA's pet theory on UFOs was confirmed, and with no less a personage than President Eisenhower in attendance as a further witness. Gerald Light kind of gloats toward the end, writing:

> "I could not stifle a wave of pity
> that arose in my own being as I
> watched the pathetic bewilderment
> of rather brilliant brains struggling
> to make some sort of rational
> explanation which would enable
> them to retain their familiar
> theories and concepts. And I
> thanked my own destiny for
> having long ago pushed me into
> the metaphysical woods…"

The entire matter was centered on the fact that Eisenhower was absent from a February 20, 1954 press conference he'd scheduled during a Palm Springs vacation. His absence caused a bit of excitement in the press, eventually forcing White House Press Secretary James Haggerty to call an urgent late evening press conference to "solemnly" announce that the poor POTUS had knocked a cap off a tooth while eating some fried chicken earlier that evening, requiring emergency treatment from a local dentist. Ike was back in time for the Sunday church service the next morning.

Critics of the "official story" are quick to point out a lack of any mention of the dentist in the Eisenhower Library's official "Dentist" file for February 1954, a further lack of a thank you note to the dentist even though pretty much everyone else involved with the Palm Springs vacation, from ministers to florists, received such acknowledgement, and the fact that Ike had just returned from a quail hunting vacation in Georgia the week prior. By Saucer Logic, the fact that there was no official documentation for an emergency dental visit and the added fact that Ike took a vacation with his family after taking personal hunting trip the week before means Ike must have really been whisked off to a super-secret saucer meeting at Muroc AFB!

As it turns out, poor Ike did have known problems with his cap. James M. Mixson published an article entitled "A History of Dwight D. Eisenhower's Oral Health" in the November 1995 issue of *The Bulletin of the History of Dentistry*. According to the records of the US Surgeon General, a porcelain cap on the president's upper left center incisor gave him frequent trouble. Installed in July 1952 during his presidential campaign, it was chipped and repaired in December 1952 and then again on February 20, 1954 when Dr. Francis A. Purcell fixed him up. Mixson's article notes that "The lack of a dental record from Purcell's office has helped fuel belief in this UFO encounter." The ornery dental cap chipped one final time in July 1954, when the POTUS had it replaced with a better model, a "thin cast gold/platinum thimble crown."

As for Gerald Light, there is the troubling fact that he really did consider the etheric a legitimate part of reality; more than one critic has suggested that it is more probable that his visit to Muroc AFB was an out-of-the-body affair rather than an actual, physical experience. The fact that this group utilizes mediums and psychics is an automatic red flag for any Bible-affirming Christian. The Bible makes it clear in passages such as Leviticus 19:31 (and many, many others) that such practices are forbidden and those who consort with spirits are to be avoided, precisely because they are messing with demonic forces.

While the Etheric view of flying saucer technically predates the abductee and contactee movement, it is interesting that the entities the BSRA were in contact with predicted the advent of flying saucers. Since Scripture reveals that God alone can predict the future [cp. Isaiah 46:9–10 & Deuteronomy 18:21-22], we can assume that these entities either created the lights and objects in the sky themselves (i.e., a self-fulfilling prophecy) or that they co-opted an existing phenomena and gave it a false or misleading explanation. Since the predictions of these beings have often failed to come to pass and, furthermore, many of their "revelations" have proven to be outright lies (e.g., Eisenhower meeting aliens), we can logically conclude that these lying spirits are not from God!

Tim Chaffey of Midwest Apologetics has suggested

that the timing of the modern UFO phenomenon and the prophetic fulfillment of the rebirth of Israel in 1948 may be significant. The return of the Jewish people to their historic homeland is widely considered one of the most important events on the prophetic timetable to the promised Second Coming of Christ. While the Arnold sighting predated the rebirth of Israel by 11 months, momentum had obviously been building up since the end of World War II. Noting that Jesus thrice mentioned in Matthew 24 that an increase in spiritual deception would occur before His return, Chaffey asks, "Is it just coincidence that an intensified demonic deception in the form of [the UFO phenomenon] sprang up as it became obvious that the nation of Israel would once again be on the face of the earth?[8]"

Men in Black II

When Gray Barker wrote about the Men in Black in *They Knew Too Much About Flying Saucers* (1956), Albert K. Bender was still maintaining his silence. Though Barker insinuated that the MIB could be something else entirely, by most accounts, the Men in Black were thought to be members of some secret government organization. Perhaps even several different ones. The FBI, Air Force and CIA were the usual suspects.

In 1962, Bender broke his silence, producing a book called *Flying Saucers and the Three Men* that claimed to finally tell the real story behind the shutdown of the International Flying Saucer Bureau in 1953. Not even Gray Barker, who published Bender's book, seemed to believe it. The MIB were retconned from shadowy government agents to something of a cross between extraterrestrials and the dero of the Shaver Mystery fame. Bender's MIB were essentially extraterrestrial agents who secretly looked like the Flatwoods Monster and were covering up the fact that they were here to collect a rare element from the Earth's oceans from their base in Antarctica. Since the project was now over and the aliens were gone, Bender was finally free to talk about it.

A book review, by Riley Crabb of the BSRA, included the following:

> "The road to hell is paved with good intentions, and in March 1953 Albert Bender was on the way in high gear. He knows now, as does many another enthusiastic Saucer researcher, and occult dabbler, that good intentions are not enough to protect one from Lucifer spirits and other Elemental forces.
>
> "When Bender's Visitors had departed his consciousness at 6:05 p.m. they left their telltale calling cards."

He then quotes from Bender's book:

"I was left puzzled by the smell of sulphur which lingered in my room for two days afterward. This smell had accompanied the other experiences (his splitting headaches, his radio turned on) and had been the most physical part of them. This time I opened my windows and used room sprays to get rid of the odor, but this did not completely dispel it. When I went to bed I could smell it in the bed clothes."

Crabb made it clear that he felt Bender had dabbled with dark occult forces and scared himself straight out of Ufology and all the rest, which is possible (if his account is true anyway). Of course, headaches, hallucinations, and a smell of sulphur can also be symptoms of epilepsy.

Nevertheless, after Bender's occultic recasting of the MIB, the idea of MIB as extraterrestrials or even ultraterrestrials began to build a following.

The modern-day cinematic portrayal of the Men in Black as government agents protecting the world from the secret of the reality of extraterrestrials owes more to Barker's book and the Men in Black comic book series created and written by Lowell Cunningham than Bender's revision.

Doctrines of Fallen Angels

It must be pointed out that there is no essential

difference between the entities these mediums communicate with and the fallen angels who communicated "new revelations" to the founders of the Islamic and Mormon faiths.

The Bible expressly warns us that the Devil can appear as an angel of light [2 Corinthians 11:14] and that even if an angel delivers a different gospel, we are to reject it [Galatians 1:8].

In the case of Islam, the angelic revelation denied the deity of Christ and holds him as a mere prophet. In the case of Mormonism, the false revelation of angels includes the idea that Jesus (and the Father) had to learn also how to become a God "the same as all Gods have done before," which directly contradicts the Biblical revelation that speak of the Tri-unity and eternal nature of the Godhead. This revelation would also make God a liar since it is written several times over in the book of Isaiah [viz., 43:11;44:6;45:5] that He expressly said that "Besides Me, there are no other gods." Mormonism also teaches that the throne of God is located near the planet Kolob and that the Earth was once located near this planet, but after its 6000 year creation period it was moved to its present position. Both the 1978 and 2003 *Battlestar Galactica* series reflect these Mormon elements. Created by Mormon Glen A. Larson, the series has it than man originated on the planet Kobol, an anagram of Kolob.

Speaking of angels, some of the Nordic aliens of the Contactee movement of the '40s and '50s have been likened to "techno-angels." Certainly, their physical appearance, in stark contrast to the cold ugliness of the Greys, was described as angelic. Like the angels of Mormonism and Islam, some of these techno-angels delivered a religious message that seemed to single out Christianity in particular. The alleged teachings of these proposed entities undermined the authority of Scripture and the deity of Christ in particular. I say alleged teachings because, honestly, we have no way of knowing whether the contactees were actually in communication with any entities or whether they were just making it up. I know that some Christian teachers tend to assume that the false teaching of the contactees are evidence that they're speaking with fallen angels who are feeding them the "doctrines of demons," but that's a pretense that ignores the fact that people come up with crazy doctrinal ideas on our own all the time. History is filled with heresies without so much as a hint of supernatural contact.

Contactee George Van Tassel claimed in *The Council of Seven Lights* (1958):

> "The space people of the Adamic race, serving as agents of God, have through the centuries followed a pattern of cycles in bringing their qualified teachers to the people of Earth. Approximately every 2100 years the spacecraft of the space people have landed one of their Divine Mothers on Earth, to give birth to a

"true son of God". As far as the records go, they have all been "virgin mothers". During the last Major Cycle the space people landed twelve teachers. The teacher called Jesus was the twelfth and last of the "sons of God" in the past Major Cycle."

He said he learned these things by channeling a being named Ashtar. Ashtar was apparently not content at merely slandering the Virgin Birth and the deity of Christ. Van Tassel's book also makes the claims that the Original Sin was miscegenation: that the Adamic space people had sex with the "animal" (but not apes; he believed it was a race above apes) race of Eve. Van Tassel blamed all of our faults on the remnants of Eve's animal nature in our bloodline.

His views on Noah and his children took this point further to outright racism. In the following passage when Van Tassel speaks of an "arc," he is speaking of a transition period between "densities," which are basically periods of time:

"Of course there was a flood during the time of the "arc of Noe". The Bible is correct when it said all the water was in the firmament (in the First density). That was why the vegetation was so thick in the First density. The moisture would condense and water the vegetation at night and rise as fog in the daytime. When the Earth flipped on its poles in the "arc of Noe", the rotational speed changed and the new temperature of the Earth being less, the waters condensed and fell from the atmosphere and flooded the land. The Bible says the waters were fifteen cubits deep (about 27 feet) in Genesis, 7: 20."

We stop here to remind our readers that he is invoking the now discredited Vapor Canopy theory which was once espoused by some Young Earth Creationists. More importantly, Genesis 7:20 actually says that the Flood waters covered the mountains by about fifteen cubits, which is much deeper than he implies here.

"So the story in the Bible of the ark and its animal cargo, is a badly twisted version of a man and a boat. ...Then the story gets further off. They confused the accurate, ancient records with another "arc". This was when the Bible story puts Noah's sons in the same boat. The animals were landed in the "arc of Noe", between the First and Second densities. Three hundred and twelve thousand years later Ham, Shem, and Japheth were landed on Earth; between the

Second and Third densities, in the "arc of Spae". Noah's "sons" were not individuals either. The race of Ham were the black people. The race of Shem were white people, and the race of Japheth were the yellow people. The various tribes that descended from these three original colors of people, that were colonized on Earth by the space people, is listed in Genesis, chapter 10. Each race is pure in its own color. And the Universal law reads "each seed after its own kind". In all the creations on the Earth, each flower, tree, animal and all of nature follows this Law-except humans who were given the right to choose. Humans were given the intelligence to raise themselves, yet humans are the only creatures that violate this Law."

First of all, you should know that Acts 17:26 teaches that all of mankind is of "one blood," so Van Tassel's teaching is definitely as unbiblical as it is racist. Even his reference to Genesis 10 and its Table of Nations fails him, for careful study reveals that many Hamitic people (like the descendants of his son Canaan, the Egyptians, many Chinese) are not dark-skinned; likewise, many dark-skinned people are descendants of Shem.

Concerning our Blessed Hope and salvation in general, Van Tassel (or the being he channeled; you choose), stated:

> "Every day that passes, you, individually, are establishing your right to be taken by the way you live. You are manifesting your choice by your actions and thinking. Each person adds increase to their vibratory body aura by conforming to the laws of the universe. Your aura, or the frequency of the body force field, will determine whether you are taken or left. A definite vibration will be established in the force field surrounding each spacecraft that will pick up people. If your body aura or force field conforms with, or exceeds, the established level of the spacecraft force field, then you can enter the ships. Remember, you are now qualifying or disqualifying yourself to be taken aboard. None can qualify another. **Jesus can't "save" you** (emphasis mine).

So, in essence, Van Tassel preached a works based salvation in which the death, burial and resurrection of Jesus Christ was completely unnecessary; If you get your aura right, by good works and thoughts, the space people will take you before this world is cleansed.

Of course, the Bible preaches something else entirely. It makes it clear that faith in the substitutionary death, burial and resurrection of Jesus Christ is the only means of eternal salvation [cp. 1 Corinthians 15; John 14:6; Acts 4:12; Romans 5:12-21] and that we are saved by grace through faith, not works that we do [John 3:16; Ephesians 2:8-10; Hebrews 11:6].

George Van Tassel isn't the only contactee who claims to have received a message from these "technological angels" that contradicts Biblical revelation. The Raelian UFO cult teaches that life on Earth was created by extraterrestrials called the Elohim (a name for the Biblical God) who arrived aboard the spacecraft called the Yahweh (yet another name for the Biblical God). They deny the existence of any god or an ethereal soul that exists outside of the body. They believe advanced Raelian supercomputers are recording our memories and DNA, and that we will be resurrected at the Apocalypse or Revelation, for judgment, after which the aliens will share their advanced knowledge. Basically they believe we can live on through transhumanism. Obviously, the Bible says that every man will give an account to God, not a bunch of extraterrestrials who claim to be so advanced, but couldn't convey Earth's history correctly (or without contradicting themselves) even though they had at least five major religions to work with.

Other unBiblical ideas propagated by the Raelian "Church" include the belief that the Garden of Eden was a large laboratory located on an artificially constructed continent, that the Great Flood was caused by the explosion from a nuclear missile fired by the Elohim, that Noah's Ark was a spaceship that carried genetic material used to resurrect animals through cloning, that the Tower of Babel was a rocket, that the Elohim contacted Jesus, John the Baptist, most of the Old Testament prophets, Joseph Smith, Mohammed and others to be their prophets, and that the aliens helped to establish the big three monotheistic religions (Judaism, Christianity and Islam), as well as Mormonism and Buddhism.

Some contactees also propagate a belief in past lives and reincarnation. The Bible states that it is appointed unto man once to die, after which comes the judgment [Hebrews 9:27], leaving no room for such a concept.

Of course, channeling itself, whether the medium believes they are the mouthpiece of spiritual or extraterrestrial intelligences is forbidden by the Bible [cp. Deuteronomy 18:11-13; Leviticus 19:31; 20:6; Galatians 1:8; 1 Timothy 4:1].

In a statement dated December 18, 1986, Ufologist William Steinman wrote his summary of the UFO or flying saucer problem. He concluded:

> "The Flying Saucers originate
> from an 'eternal dimension',
> subject to space and time, as we

know it" and that they
"'materialize' out of this 'eternal dimension' into our space time frame, and have been doing so since time immemorial." Furthermore, he deduced "a direct relationship between 'The Great Secret' of the Occult teachings, 'The Mystery of Iniquity' of the Bible, and the Flying Saucer Phenomena" and identified the "'Dark Forces' of the Occult, summed up as Satan (Lucifer) in the Bible" as the "underlying source behind the Flying Saucer Phenomena."

The idea that the one the Bible refers to as the "Prince of the power of the air" [Ephesians 2:2] would be behind the UFO phenomenon is certainly the most popular amongst Christians.

It's also popular amongst some non-Christian Ufologists. John Keel leaned toward a supernatural explanation, noting that:

> "The UFOs do not seem to exist as tangible, manufactured objects. They do not conform to the accepted natural laws of our environment. They seem to be nothing more than transmogrifications tailoring themselves to our abilities to

understand. The thousands of contacts with the entities indicate that they are liars and put-on artists. The UFO manifestations seem to be, by and large, merely minor variations of the age-old demonological phenomenon.[9]"

Indeed, one of the other reasons why some have come to the conclusion that UFOs must be supernatural (either etheric or angelic) in nature is the fact that they seem to materialize out of thin air and vanish just as inexplicably, they usually don't show up on radar and are capable of movements that seem to defy our very notions of physics. One of the terms Meade Layne's occult organization first referred to UFOs by was "etheric aeroforms." They believed that UFOs inhabited a different plane of existence or dimension and that they could "mat" and "demat" (materialize and dematerialize) in our plane of existence by use of the correct frequencies. To the Christian, this sounds suspiciously like accounts of angelic visitation. To be fair, it also sounds like one of *Star Trek*'s transporters.

Keel isn't the only Ufologist to make the connection that the entities posing as extraterrestrials in these tales have much in common with demons.

Lynn E. Catoe, senior biographer for the Library of Congress, wrote the following in the Preface of a document on UFOs written for the US Air Force under AFOSR project orders 67-0002 and 68-0003:

"A large part of the available UFO literature is closely linked with mysticism and the metaphysical. It deals with subjects like mental telepathy, automatic writing, and invisible entities as well as phenomena like poltergeist manifestations and "possession." One school of thought holds that flying saucers are Biblical "signs in the sky" that portend the Second Coming. Another believes that an invisible fourth- or other-dimensional world is involved. Some groups have concluded that mankind is being, and may have always been, manipulated by extraterrestrial forces -- the UFO occupants. Others detail the endless battle between "good" and "evil' believing that the UFOs play an integral part in this "war." Unearthly "police forces" are described and explained.[10]

Many of the UFO abduction reports now being published in the popular press recount alleged incidents that are strikingly similar to demoniac possession and psychic phenomena which have long been known to theologians and parapsychologists."

There are several points of similarity between alien abductions and reported accounts of demonic activity. For example, anecdotal accounts of demonic activity include telepathic communication, loss of consciousness, and psychic abduction episodes involving paralysis, rape, molestation and physical suffering. Supernatural manifestations may occur, like levitation, going into a trance, becoming a mouthpiece for the entity or so-called "poltergeist" or psychokinetic activity.

Some folks are attracted to the supernatural or ultraterrestrial hypothesis because of its superior explanatory power if contrasted with the extraterrestrial hypothesis. For example, there is a glaring contrast between the early contactee tales of benevolent Space Brothers and modern abductee accounts wherein victims are subjected to crude medical and genetic procedures without their permission. The Space Brothers were allegedly here to warn us of impending doom (even if we apparently had to save ourselves). There seems to be no motive for abduction accounts by the so-called Greys, aside from base sadism. The demeanor and description of the aliens isn't the only difference between the contactee and abductee scenarios. Contactees generally feel drawn to go to some remote location (think of Roy Neary, Richard Dreyfuss' character in *Close Encounters of the Third Kind*) and experience no loss of time. One has to wonder what happened here. I mean, why was there a shift from benevolent Space Brothers spewing New Age deception to traumatic secret abductions by

Greys?

I'm reminded again of how Tim Chaffey suggested a possible significance in the timing of the advent of UFO phenomenon and the prophesied rebirth of Israel in 1948. If he's on the right track, might there not be a similar explanation for the contactee/abductee shift? The abduction movement began with the Hill Abduction in 1961.

The primary objections to the contactee movement were a general lack of proof of the experiences, the cult-like zeal with which contactees spread the religious messages of the Space Brothers, the fact that the aliens claimed to be from Mars, Venus and Saturn when scientists were increasingly determining that those places were inhospitable to life, and the fact that the aliens were human-looking. The latter point flew in the face of evolutionary beliefs about alien life. It stretches credulity too far to suggest that convergent evolution could account for species that allegedly developed on completely separate planets with no common ancestor that are nonetheless exactly alike in appearance.

That is not to say that evolutionists aren't already suggesting that convergent evolution result in intelligent creatures that greatly resemble humans. In his 2015 book, *The Runes of Evolution*, Professor Simon Conway[11] argues that convergent evolution is "completely ubiquitous," so that "the things which we regard as most important, ie cognitive sophistication, large brains, intelligence, tool making, are also convergent. Therefore, in principle, other Earth-like planets should very much end up with the same sort of arrangement."

Dr. Jacques Vallee[12], one of the pioneers of UFO research and the inspiration for the character of Claude Lacombe in Steven Spielberg's *Close Encounters of the Third Kind,* has said:

> "No serious investigator has ever been very worried by the claims of the 'contactees.'"

The irony is that his observation does not extend to Christian investigators. Christian Ufologists do worry about the claims of contactees, because they worry that the source of their New Age religious messages is very real (just not extraterrestrial). While the contactees have been thoroughly discredited, the Christian has to wonder if there's a connection between the anti-Christian messages of the alleged Nordic aliens of the contactees and the equally anti-Christian messages of the alleged Grey aliens of the abductee movement. And if fallen angels are at the root of both as some suspect, why did they change their tactics?

We must point out that the abduction scenario is more in line with modern science. At the very least, it's not obviously false. The Space Race had just begun in earnest. We'd just seen the launch of Sputnik in 1957. On May 25, 1961, US President John F. Kennedy made his famous promise to put a man on the moon by the end of the decade. Four months later, the first alleged alien abduction occurs.

With this in mind, we ask ourselves: If a fair portion of the UFO phenomenon is demonic, could the timing of the abduction movement with the beginning of the Space Race be significant? If fallen angels decided to alter their tactics in regards to the UFO deception in order to maintain some semblance of credibility, it suggests that they consider the UFO angle potentially useful – at least enough so that the salvage attempt was worth it.

While the abduction scenario is more in line with the times, that does not mean I find it any less believable than the contactee claims. I mean, if we seriously examine the extraterrestrial hypothesis in light of abductee claims, I think we do have to ask ourselves why aliens would expend the resources to travel all the way to earth, as prohibitive as that is, only to sneak into people's bedrooms, kidnap them and take them on spaceships so they can conduct invasive, traumatic medical experiments on them? When does that start making sense? And if their tech is so advanced, why the medieval medical procedures? In all seriousness, most alien abduction scenarios are pretty scary. I mean, why anal probes? Why??

West Virginia native Budd Hopkins, dubbed the "father of the modern abduction movement," popularized the idea of alien abductions as genetic experiments through his 1987 book, *Intruders: The Incredible Visitations at Copley Woods*. Hopkins likens abductees to rape victims[13]. He concluded, based on their oft-times nightmarish experiences, that either the aliens "have not grasped the psychological toll they are taking in these abductions and genetic experiments because they really do not understand human psychology, or they must be viewed as a callous, indifferent, amoral race bent solely upon gratifying its own scientific needs at whatever the cost to us, the victims.[14]"

Dr. Jacques Vallee[15] wrote the following in his book, *Confrontations*:

> "The 'medical examination' to which abductees are said to be subjected, often accompanied by sadistic sexual manipulation, is reminiscent of the medieval tales of encounters with demons. It makes no sense in a sophisticated or technical framework: any intelligent being equipped with the scientific marvels that UFOs possess would be in a position to achieve any of these alleged scientific objectives in a shorter time and with fewer risks."

In either case, space travel across vasty distances seems a prohibitive venture for any group of beings, meaning that their technology would be far advanced of ours…so why would they string out their conquest of a technologically inferior race by hiding for years in the background, positioning themselves as some sort of vast subversive alien conspiracy? I think you see my point.

Unlike angelic visitations in the Bible, no one's telling abductees to "Fear not" – and none of these alleged "aliens" are really up front about what they're doing. Without our permission. Those methods – invasive, traumatic, secretive, terrifying – that sounds like the work of the *other* guys: you know, demons, fallen angels, the Devil. It's little wonder why so many Christians suppose that Satan must be largely responsible for the modern UFO deception!

John Ankerberg and John Weldon point out that another, more disturbing trend of both the contactee and abductee movements, namely the lies they communicate:

> "...Further, in light of the messages given by the UFO entities, how credible is it to think that literally thousands of genuine extraterrestrials would fly millions or billions of light years simply to teach New Age philosophy, deny Christianity, and support the occult? Why would they do this with the preponderance of such activity already occurring on this planet? And why would the entities actually possess and inhabit people (as in Walk-ins and channeling) just like demons do if they were really advanced extraterrestrials? Why would they

consistently lie about things which we know are true, and why would they purposely deceive their contacts?[16]"

More than one contactee has been promised that if they told their story, the Space Brothers would confirm it later which, of course, has never, ever happened. Likewise, no prophecy credited to an alleged extraterrestrial entity has ever come true. Meade Layne was well aware that his Etherians were capable of hoaxing him. Both contactees and abductees have been told that Jesus was an alien (or a hybrid), some version of a future alien "Rapture," or that aliens created life on Earth. There also seems to be a humanist aspect to their messages; that is, they preach that some impending disaster is upon mankind, but they never lift a finger to help us. Mankind must come together and save himself! In plain speech, this resonates with the concept of the autonomy of man.

A lot of Christians also worry about the idea of aliens and UFOs because they fear that people will see extraterrestrials as a surrogate savior. It's true that some folks that some of the folks obsessed with aliens suppose that aliens will bring with them a storehouse of advanced knowledge. In their minds, aliens could give us advanced technology and medical knowledge to erase poverty, hunger, disease and maybe even death itself.

The absolute biggest reason why many Christians see the UFO phenomenon as 100% demonic is what is often called the "unwanted piece of the UFO puzzle." A group of Christian abduction researchers called the CE4 Research Group[17] (who get their name from Close Encounters of the 4th Kind, another term for alien abduction) found that Christian alien abduction experiences could be stopped cold simply by invoking the name and authority of Jesus!

All of these factors read like giant red flags to any Bible-affirming Christian.

Yet I cannot agree with Christian abduction researcher Jefferson Scott that "the UFO phenomenon is 100% demonic," precisely because I think the evidence suggests there is no magic bullet for the UFO question. In other words, there is no one-size-fits-all theory. Are some abduction accounts demonic in nature? Probably. Are some psychological? Undoubtedly. And some are probably hoaxes and outright frauds. If the law of mediocrity holds, the vast majority of unidentified are simply mundane terrestrial phenomena that we never gained sufficient evidence to properly identify.

The "unwanted piece of the UFO puzzle" is just that: one piece. While I do not doubt the efficacy of the name of Jesus to cast out demons, I must submit that the efficacy of the name of Jesus is not limited to demons. The calling upon the name of Jesus could just as easily stop an hallucination or nightmare as an actual demonic experience. In fact, in the same article wherein Jefferson Scott stated his belief that the UFO phenomenon is 100% demonic, he also stated the following[18]:

"I'm not saying these encounters aren't real. I'm not even saying they are completely psychological. But I am suggesting there may be a significant hallucinatory component to these events. I believe the mind is a large part of (if not 90% of) the playing field for "close encounters.""

The trouble with fantastic explanations of the UFO phenomenon as a whole is that they tend to be emphasized over more natural explanations. Now, as a Christian, I obviously accept the supernatural as valid.

In my book *Defending Genesis*, I noted the following:

"If God exists, there exists the possibility that some problems will require a supernatural answer.

"Now, this is not to say that all problems will require a supernatural answer [an appeal to God, if you will] or that no problems will have natural explanations. Given the intricacy and complexity of design observable in nature, but also the inter-relatedness of its systems, laws, ecologies and species, (and in light of the promise of the uniformity of nature given in Genesis 8:22) we should expect to see that a majority of the problems shall have natural solutions. To put it another way, since the supernatural [God] has set up the natural world and its laws, processes, et cetera, and since we observe the natural world we inhabit and have limited or no access to the supernatural [here, being that which exists outside the natural] apart from God's will and revelation, we should expect that most solutions of the natural world shall be natural.

"Even so, if the world has a supernatural designer, a minority of data and problems shall certainly require a supernatural explanation [again, if God does indeed exist].[19]"

In other words, given what we observe of the world, supernatural activity is the exception rather than the rule. Most solutions to the problems we attempt to solve will be natural.

Yet some Christians, influenced by books like Gary Bates' *Alien Intrusion*, tend to see the contactee/abductee phenomenon as pretty much synonymous with the work of fallen angels and demonic forces. For example, Christian abduction researcher Jefferson Scott states that "the UFO phenomenon is 100% demonic." While I admit an element of the occult exists in the UFO phenomenon, I submit that his conclusion is unlikely to be the case. If the law of mediocrity holds, demonic activity accounts for a minimum of these cases, at best.

Again, those who see the Devil behind every abduction account would do well to recall what C.S. Lewis observed in *The Screwtape Letters*, that it is equal error to make too much or too little of the Devil.

Christian culture warriors like Bob Larson made much of the Devil in the 1980s. He and teachers like him convinced many that demons were hiding in their music and all sorts of other stuff. This excessive emphasis on the demonic even caused some believers to wonder if Christians could be demon possessed! The truth of the matter is that the Devil might be the prince of this world, but he is not God. He lacks God's power, foresight, wisdom, omniscience, omnipresence and pretty much everything else that makes God *God*. In other words, Satan is neither all-wise nor all-powerful. He does not know the future. He is not everywhere; only God is omnipresent. Neither does the Devil know the future, for true prophecy is the province of God alone. Furthermore, if Revelation 12:4 is an indication of the number of the angelic hosts which fell with Satan, he is twice outnumbered by the heavenly hosts alone. Neither can the Devil do whatever he pleases, if the Book of Job is any indication. The Devil is no match for God. In this fact, the Christian takes consolation and confidence.

So it's not all the Devil anyway. Even giving the Devil his due, it's not even Ol' Slewfoot most of the time. Most of the time, it's something else entirely, but I'm sure that snake doesn't mind taking the credit anyway.

In fact, it does seem apparent that while the UFO phenomenon is not 100% demonic, the Devil has appropriated large segments of the UFO phenomenon to undermine the authority of the Bible and deceive folks into New Age religious beliefs. So it is perhaps with good intentions that some of my fellow Christians paint the UFO phenomenon with a broad brush; however, the distinction between source and utility is important for at least one good reason.

When we tell folks that this UFO thing is 100% demonic, we do so out of a desire to warn folks of the dangers inherent in much of the contactee/abductee messages and false Ancient Astronaut type claims about the Bible and Earth's history, but we're going about it the wrong way. It's the truth that sets folks free. Truth is not found in overstatement. The truth is that most – and by most, we mean the overwhelming majority – of the UFO phenomenon has a mundane answer. The truth is that many of these UFO-related claims contradict the teachings of the Bible, the latter of which is a trusted authority which has been supernaturally authenticated by fulfilled prophecy. The message of the "aliens" has no such authentications. Every prophecy they've uttered has failed.

***

Notes

1. Dash, Mike. *Borderlands: The Ultimate Exploration of the Unknown*. Delta (2000), p. 228.

2. Kripal, Jeffrey J., *Mutants and Mystics: Science Fiction, Superhero Comics, and the Paranormal*. University of Chicago Press (2011), p.103.

3. Richard Shaver's wife Dottie claims that he did come to believe in God during the last 18 days of his life. As cited in Toronto, Richard. *War Over Lemuria: Richard Shaver, Ray Palmer and the Strangest Chapter of 1940s Science Fiction*. McFarland (2013), p. 235.

4. Kripal, *Ibid*.

5. Layne, Meade. "Welcome, Kareeta!" *Round Robin* Vol 2. No. 10 (October 1946), pp.3-7.

6. Ray Palmer was certainly familiar with Meade Layne's organization. Perhaps this "Kareeta's return" is what Ray Palmer was referring to when he "predicted" the advent of the saucers in the April 1947 issue of *Amazing Stories*.

7. Layne, Meade. "FLY, LOKAS, FLY! (The

incursion of the 'flying saucers')." Round Robin Vol 3. No. 6. (July/August 1947), pp. 3-8.

8. Chaffey, Tim. "Q & A Series: Were the Sons of God and Nephilim Ancient Aliens?" MidwestApologetics.org. (June 23, 2011). Web. Retrieved October 15, 2016. Brackets mine for clarification. Chaffey's original sentence stated "alien abductions" instead of "the UFO phenomenon;" however the abduction movement began later in the 60s and the rest of Chaffey's article makes it clear that he means the UFO phenomenon in general.

9. Keel, John. *UFOs: Operation Trojan Horse.* Abacus (1973), p 299.

10. Catoe, Lynn E. UFOs and Related Subjects: An Annotated Bibliography, Prepared by the Library of Congress, July 1969. In his 2004 book, Alien Intrusion, Gary Bates provides an incomplete quotation of this passage as cited from "The Premise of Spiritual Warfare In Relation to Alien Abductions" by Wesley M. Clark, which likewise lacked ellipses indicating the omission. I'm not sure why Bates truncated the title to "The Premise of Spiritual Warfare" in his Chapter 8 Notes, as the Wayback Machine indicates that the title of Clark's article was never altered in any way.

11. Gallagher, Paul. "Forget little green men – aliens will look like humans, says Cambridge University evolution expert." Independent.co.uk. Web (July 1, 2015).

12. Vallee, Jacques. *Anatomy of a Phenomenon: Unidentified Objects in Space, A Scientific Appraisal*. Henry Regnery Company (1965), p.90.

13. Hopkins, Budd. "Ethical implications of the UFO abduction phenomenon." (September 1987). Web. http://www.bibliotecapleyades.net/vida_alien/alien_abductionabductees22.htm. Retrieved May 18, 2016.

14. *Ibid.*

15. Vallee, Jacques. *Confrontations: A Scientist's Search for Alien Contact*. Ballantine Books (1990), p. 17.

16. Ankerberg, John & John Weldon, *The Facts on UFOs and Other Supernatural Phenomena*. Harvest House (1992), .p. 13.

17. Visit AlienResistance.org to find out more about how the name of Jesus stops alien abductions.

18. Scott, Jefferson. "UFOs and the Christian Worldview." JeffersonScott.com. Web. Retrieved July 21, 2016.

19. Breeden, Tony. *Defending Genesis: How We Got Here & Why It Matters.* (2015), p.88. Yes, it is weird quoting myself.

Tony Breeden

11 UFOs and the Bible

It should not surprise us that some members of the UFO community have attempted to misappropriate the Bible to their cause. John Keel stated the following in *UFOs: Operation Trojan Horse*[1]:

> "Like most UFO researchers, I have read the Bible carefully several times. In view of what we now know~or suspect-about flying saucers, many of the Biblical accounts of things in the sky take on a new meaning and even corroborate some of the things happening today. They were given a religious interpretation in those ancient days when all natural phenomena and all catastrophes were blamed on a Superior Being.
>
> Today we kneel before the altar of science; and our scientific ignorance receives the blame for what we do not know or cannot understand. The game's the same, only the rules have changed slightly."

When we look at any subject as Christians, the first place we should look is the Bible. Which begs the question: Does the Bible say anything about aliens or flying saucers?

Yes and no.

As we discussed earlier, there is a distinct difference between a flying saucer and a UFO, the latter of which is quite literally something you see in the sky that you can't quite identify.

Ufologists often cite Ezekiel's wheel as a UFO. In the strictest sense of the word, Ezekiel's wheel is certainly a UFO. I mean, what is a "wheel within a wheel" anyway, right? I'm not sure I'd be able to identify that. The Biblical description certainly resonates with folks who obsess over strange lights in the sky that change direction at sharp angles:

> "And when I looked, behold the four wheels by the cherubims, one wheel by one cherub, and another wheel by another cherub: and the appearance of the wheels was as the colour of a beryl stone.
>
> And as for their appearances, they four had one likeness, as if a wheel had been in the midst of a wheel.
>
> When they went, they went upon their four sides; they turned not as they went, but to the place whither the head looked they followed it; they turned not as they went."
> [Ezekiel 10:9-11]

Of course, unlike a classic saucer sighting, these wheels were accompanied by angelic beings (cherubim). Furthermore, the wheels followed the cherubim, mimicking their flight exactly. It should be said that Ezekiel was a prophet and he was likely seeing a supernatural vision akin to the valley of dry bones rather than reality [Ezekiel 37:1-14]. *If* Ezekiel's wheel is the Biblical equivalent of a modern "saucer" sighting, one wonders if people are seeing the wheel but not the accompanying cherubim, rather like Balaam was unable to see the angel sent to kill him [Number 22:31] and Elisha's servant was unable to see the heavenly hosts [2 Kings 6:17] until their respective eyes were opened to the spiritual reality. It's certainly the only compelling Biblical parallel we have to the modern phenomenon of UFO sightings.

Of course, if we were to concede the idea that Ezekiel's wheel was a flying saucer, it begs the question posed by Captain James T. Kirk in *Star Trek V: The Final Frontier* (1989): "What does God need with a starship?"

One could conceivably counter this question with an appeal to Arthur C. Clarke's Third Law ("Any sufficiently advanced technology is indistinguishable from magic."). In fact, skeptic Michael Shermer has formulated a corollary called Shermer's Last Law, which half-jokingly suggests that "Any sufficiently advanced ETI (extraterrestrial intelligence) is indistinguishable from God." The entire concept is an assumption that God is not supernatural so much as sufficiently advanced as to appear so.

While some Ufologists and UFO cults have

suggested that God is in fact an extraterrestrial, this is hard to support from a purely Biblical perspective. If God is merely an advanced alien, he must also be a time traveler, for the Bible is rather big on fulfilled prophecy. A bigger problem with the notion of God as an alien is that he would be bound by the laws of the universe, including the space-time continuum, which would mean He is not eternal, as the Bible claims.

Other alleged claims to Biblical support for UFOs include:

- Aliens brought life to Earth, either directly or by seeding life throughout the universe (i.e. panspermia).
- Aliens directed the evolution of our ape-like ancestors, resulting in Adam and Eve.
- Angels are aliens
- The "Sons of God" of Genesis 6 are aliens and the Nephilim are alien hybrids.
- Enoch was abducted.
- Flying saucers destroyed Sodom and Gomorrah with Martian death rays or nukes or whatever.
- The pillar of cloud and fire that guided the Israelites through the desert as a flying saucer.
- Flying saucers dropped manna from heaven for the Israelites to eat.

- Elijah's fiery chariot as a UFO... but, let's be honest, the added presence of fiery horses [2 Kings 2:11] kind of make that a stretch. Especially when the heavenly hosts show up with these same chariots and horses in connection with Elisha [2 Kings 6:17].

- The Star of Bethlehem as a flying saucer.

- The Virgin Mary was artificially inseminated by extraterrestrials resulting in an advanced Child with extraterrestrial powers. Yeah... That's just far beyond disrespectful; it's blasphemy. But this is what you get when folks believe in aliens but refuse to consider the possibility that a supernatural God exists. Meanwhile, the first chapter of the Gospel of John makes it clear that Christ is also the Creator of the cosmos, not merely an advanced inhabitant of it.

- Jesus was beamed up by a flying saucer at His Ascension.

- The Apostle Paul was abducted by aliens when he was "caught up in the third heaven."

There's no evidence for any of these claims. It's just a saucerian re-interpretation of the text that presumes that aliens have been visiting this Earth with impunity for a long, long time (and not just since Kenneth Arnold's 1947 sighting), so there must be evidence for it in the past. In order to fit the Bible into their saucer-shaped hole, they must conclude that the Bible is not the inspired supernatural revelation of God but rather the work of fallible men who mistook the acts of aliens as evidence of a Deity. The trouble with this is that the revelation of the Bible is supernaturally authenticated by fulfilled prophecy and the Resurrection of Christ; no other truth claim can equal this claim to authority and veracity as the very Word of God.

Admittedly, one of the reasons they're convinced that the Ancient Astronaut scenario is true is because of the genius of ancient man. According to the standard evolutionary timeline, mankind slowly evolved from his ape-like ancestors over a long period of time. He is assumed to be too primitive to have created the Great Pyramid of Giza, Stonehenge, Pumapunku, or the Antikythera mechanism. For example, as early as 1955, Morris K. Jessup stated that the Great Pyramid "embodies more astronomy and mathematics than was possessed by those people to whom its construction is attributed." *Edison's Conquest of Mars*, a space opera written as a serial by Garrett P. Serviss in 1898, and published as a book in 1947, was the first science fiction work to feature aliens building the pyramids.

Aliens are invoked to account for the assumed "need" for more advanced technology. By contrast, the Bible records that Adam was created fully mature and with an intellect advanced enough to comprehend language. Genesis 4:20-22 relates that the Pre-Flood world included men such as "Jabal: he was the father of such as dwell in tents, and of such as have cattle. And his brother's name was Jubal: he was the father of all such as handle the harp and organ. And ...Tubalcain, an instructer of every artificer in brass and iron." So according to the Bible, the Antediluvian world included metalworking, among other skills. If the Bible's history is true (and considering the supernatural authentication of fulfilled Bible prophecy, I have no reason to doubt its veracity), it appears we lost skills along the way and then rediscovered them later in history.

Lifespans recorded for men before the Flood are notably longer than Post-Flood. A variety of reasons have been suggested for the decrease in lifespans, chief among them a genetic bottleneck and a transformed environment due to the Flood itself. In any case, if men lived for hundreds of years as the Bible records, their knowledge must have been vast. Noah and his family would have only been able to bring a portion of that accumulated Antediluvian knowledge with them aboard the Ark.

The Ark Encounter in Williamstown, KY, features a Biblically accurate life-size Ark containing various exhibits on the Flood of Noah's day. One of the exhibits is Noah's library, featuring cabinets filled with rolled parchments and a few clay tablets. It's possible that Noah recorded some of the knowledge of the pre-Flood world in this manner, if writing was one of the advances pioneered by the Antediluvian world.

Charles Kimball[2] has suggested that the absence of written language in out-of-place artifacts (OOPArts) from the Antediluvian suggests that there might be some truth to a tale told by Socrates in Plato's *Phaedrus* concerning the Egyptian god Teuth (Thoth) and King Thamus. In the tale, Teuth believes that writing will be a remedy for memory, while Thamus believes that it will serve as a replacement for memory and will thus only serve to encourage forgetfulness and lax education. The sheer amount of archaeological knowledge lost in the several burnings of the Library of Alexandria and other ancient libraries testified to the cynical truth of King Thamus' prediction. In regards to our discussion, the memory of men of near-Adamic perfection must have been prodigious.

We see then that the Bible can account for the pyramids and other ancient marvels as evidence of the genius of man before he fell into more primitive states – and we can account for them without the need to appeal to aliens for which there is no smoking ray gun.

The fact of the matter is that every effort to force the Bible into a saucer-shaped hole leads to confusion and actually undermines the authority of the very Book that they are trying to say confirms their theory. Meanwhile the Bible stands as a supernatural revelation of a supernatural Creator – not an extraterrestrial – through the supernatural authentication of fulfilled Bible prophecy and the Resurrection of Christ.

Unfortunately, many of the same observations I highlighted in my book *Defending Genesis*, concerning competing paradigms applies not only to the Origins Debate but also to those who espouse the Ancient Astronaut hypothesis. In that book, I quoted Thomas Kuhn, who said:

> "[P]roponents of competing paradigms... are bound partly to talk through each other. Though each may hope to convert the other to his way of seeing science and its problems, neither may hope to prove his case. The competition between paradigms is not the sort of battle that can be resolved by proofs[3]."

In other words, it's not about the evidence; it's about the interpretation. A person who is convinced that aliens have been visiting this planet with impunity for thousands of years must needs also believe that the Bible is a flawed record that superstitiously attributed the works of extraterrestrials to imagined supernatural forces. If the Ancient Astronaut theory is true, the Bible is false. If the Bible is true, the Ancient Astronaut theory is false.

There is really no comparison. The Ancient Astronaut theory is purest speculation while the Bible is authenticated by fulfilled prophecy and the Resurrection of Jesus Christ.

Even so, there are those who will refuse to see the truth. As the Bible warns:

"For the time will come when they will not endure sound doctrine; but after their own lusts shall they heap to themselves teachers, having itching ears; And they shall turn away their ears from the truth, and shall be turned unto fables." [2 Timothy 4:3-4]

***

Notes

1. Keel, John. UFOs: Operation Trojan Horse. Abacus (1973), p 32.

2. Charles Kimball, Charles. "Chapter 9: Ten Generations," The Genesis Chronicles: A Proposed History of The Morning Of The World. *The Xenophile Historian.* Web. (xenohistorian.faithweb.com/genesis/gen09.html). Accessed October 5, 2016.

3. Kuhn, Thomas S. *The Structure of Scientific Revolutions*, 2nd Edition. University of Chicago Press (1970), p.148. Quoted in *Defending Genesis*, p. 12.

Part 3: Speculative Exotheology

12 Are We Alone?

A large number of Americans believe that extraterrestrials exist somewhere in space. A 2012 Kelton Research survey of a random sample of 1114 Americans adults found that 36% said they believed that aliens have visited the Earth, 17% said that aliens hadn't, and 77% were undecided. This survey is consistent with similar polls done in the past.

The general consensus is that, while only one-fifth to one-third of the American public thinks aliens have actually visited this planet, over half of us believe aliens exist anyway, with a quarter of us dissenting and the remainder being undecided. The takeaway message is that more people believe in the plausibility of the premise of the *X Files* than those who don't, but most of us simply think the vote's still out! Of those who do believe extraterrestrials exist, roughly two-thirds are more prone to believe that they exist somewhere *out there*, far from Earth.

Which brings up the question: Even if we all agreed that the UFOs phenomenon, including contactee tales and abduction accounts, are just cases of misidentification, hoaxes, hallucinations, and Satanic deceptions, does that mean extraterrestrials do not exist independently of the UFO phenomenon? You see, the issue of the identity of UFOs and whether aliens have visited this planet is quite independent of the question of whether extraterrestrials might exist and whether they contradict the Bible's revelation.

What would UFO accounts have to do with aliens we've never encountered living somewhere out there in the heavens? Um, nothing. If those extraterrestrials even exist, all evidence connected with the UFO mythos would have NOTHING to do with them, meaning that charges of demonic deception and all that are irrelevant to the question we are about to discuss.

NASA knows this. NASA Astrobiology Institute senior scientist David Morrison wrote the following on July 10, 2006 in response to a question posed to their Ask An Astrobiologist feature:

> "As far as I know, no claims of UFOs as being alien craft have any validity -- the claims are without substance, and certainly not proved. There are many such claims on the Internet, but no

scientific evidence to support them[1]."

I would caution Christian leaders against using emotional appeals based on the UFO phenomenon to condemn consideration of the question of extraterrestrial life in general, because this is comparing apples to oranges. It's tantamount to saying, "Aliens never visited Earth; therefore aliens don't exist at all."

In astronomy professor David Weintraub's book, *Religions and Extraterrestrial Life*[2], he notes that a 2013 survey of 5,886 Americans by consumer research firm *Survata* found that belief in extraterrestrials varies by religious affiliation: Atheists (55%), Muslims (44%), Jews (37%), Hindus (36%) and Christians (32%). Evangelicals and fundamentalists tend to be the most resistant to the idea of alien life, because they believe it contradicts the Gospel. Only 21 percent of the respondents held the position that extraterrestrial life does not exist at all.

Most of us have heard of SETI (the Search for Extraterrestrial Intelligence). If nowhere else, you've probably seen them featured in blockbuster alien invasion films like *Independence Day* (1996) and *Contact* (1997). Few realize that SETI has its origins in Project Ozma, an earlier project by Frank Drake at the National Radio Astronomy Observatory in Green Bank, West Virginia. Basically, they're a group of extra-terrestrial enthusiasts who are scanning the universe for signals which could be signs of intelligent communication. In other words, they're looking for signs of intelligent design.

The irony is that our DNA contains such information that it would qualify as the result of intelligent design; however, the modern scientific consensus is very much opposed to intelligent design theory when it might infer a supernatural Creator but they inconsistently invoke its principles when searching for extraterrestrial communications. It's fair to ask why aliens get a free pass.

There's the feeling among evolutionists that life is somehow inevitable and that chemicals spontaneously produce life which then evolves into more and more complex forms until it achieves sufficient mental complexity to be called intelligent. This is based on two things: the vastness of the universe and an unBiblical misconception as to how long the universe has been around. Put simply, evolutionists feel that there's been ample time for alien abiogenesis and evolution to occur a ridiculous number of times and given the vastness of space, we're probably just tripping over one another on a relative scale. NASA experts are now claiming we will find aliens and new Earths within the next 20 years because, as Charles Bolden (head of NASA) stated:

> "It's highly improbable in the limitless vastness of the universe that we humans stand alone[3]."

I find it interesting that they *don't* base their views on the inevitability and alleged scale of extraterrestrial life on actual probability studies. You see, abiogenesis (i.e., life springing from chemicals by natural processes) and molecules-to-man evolution are so statistically improbable as to rate impossibility. Multiplying zero by infinity doesn't really add up to better odds.

No, evolutionists are simply arguing from incredulity – "Now, doesn't all that space seem wasteful?" and the principle of mediocrity wedded to an all-natural assumption of how life originated here on Earth – "If life exists out there, it must've happened by undirected processes because like it did on Earth." And if it happened here and it was completely impossible then maybe it's not so impossible after all. Maybe it's only apparently impossible, not actually impossible – after all, evolutionists would have us also believe that we may observe apparent design in nature, but not actual design! Now I tend to think that if they had the most improbable of chances for undirected processes to lead to complex intelligent life and they multiplied it by the alleged deep time and scale of the universe that they'd would've used up all of their odds on Earth alone. To put it a different way, even if it was extremely improbable and it happened anyway, the chances of it happening again become less likely not as likely or more likely.

In his 2006 lecture, *Life in the Universe?*, Stephen Hawking suggested that maybe our expectations are too high. Perhaps the actual chances of life spontaneously happening so low that the Earth is the only place where it happened.

In his book, *Life Itself*, Francis Crick[4] wrote:

> "The origin of life appears to be almost a miracle, so many are the conditions which would have to be satisfied to get it going."

Unwilling to capitulate his reputation to the admission of the need for a Creator, he has suggested that life on Earth was seeded by aliens, an idea known as panspermia. Panspermia can be either undirected (accidental) or directed, meaning that aliens seeded us on purpose. This former idea has been amusingly spoofed in the animated short film *Monsters vs Aliens: Mutant Pumpkins from Outer Space* (2009), wherein glowing goo dumped from a flying saucer's toilet causes some rather unexpected results her eon Earth! The latter concept was illustrated in a memorable episode of *Star Trek: The Next Generation*. In "The Chase" [Season 6 Episode 20. Air date April 23, 1996] directed by cast member Jonathan Frakes, Captain Jean-Luc Picard sets off on an archaeological quest that reveals that all humanoid species in the Star Trek universe have a common humanoid ancestor who seeded these races on different worlds so that they would not be alone as the progenitor race was.

The problem with this obvious dodge is that it leads to the inevitable question of "How did alien life originate?" It goes without saying that if life was unlikely on this planet, even given the allowance of an evolutionary time scale, it is even more improbable if we first have to wait for an alien race to come to be, evolve and develop to the point where it can travel to Earth with life seeding technology.

Given the prohibitive nature of space travel, it is unlikely that man will discover life from beyond our solar system. All science fiction writers employ black boxes to overcome this obstacle (warp engines, inertial dampeners, wormholes, hyperspace, etc.), but the physics and distance make the whole venture wholly impractical. Impossible really.

Robin Hanson of George Mason University has suggested that the reason we see no other evidence of life in the universe, a puzzle called the Fermi Paradox, is that some sort of Cosmic Filter prevents life from developing past a certain stage. Australian National University astrobiologists Aditya Chopra and Charley Lineweaver believe that the Great Filter comes early. Their Gaian Bottleneck theory suggests that life evolves on other planets but goes extinct before it can develop quickly enough to regulate greenhouse gases to keep surface temperatures stable. Physicist Brian Cox believes that the Great Filter occurs later. He believes that societies that have the power to destroy themselves likely develop more quickly than controls designed to prevent that destruction. His theory is a double-edged sword, since he believes the Earth could also be headed in this direction. As a result, he believes that we will never encounter extraterrestrial life.

The idea that humanity is the first intelligent life form to evolve in the universe and that we will be the progenitor race suggested in *Star Trek: The Next Generation* episode called "The Chase" has been proffered as yet another answer to the Fermi Paradox. Given the suggested evolutionary age of the universe, this scenario seems inconsistent with their beliefs, to say the least.

In 1973, astronomer John Ball suggested the Zoo Hypothesis to answer the Fermi Paradox is astronomer John Ball's Zoo Hypothesis. This is the idea advanced aliens do exist and are in communication with one another, but that the Earth is purposely being kept in the dark by a Galactic Club because we're too primitive. Scottish astronomer Duncan Forgan tested this idea via computer simulations, noting that such an intergalactic agreement requires communication. With evidence of such communication in absence, he deduced that if aliens exist, they must exist as a smaller Clique rather than a Galactic Club. Furthermore, he said that if this is the case, either aliens do not exist locally [or at all] or we belong to a Clique that is keeping us in the dark until we reach a certain technological milestone or whatever.

I discussed another proposal to solve the Fermi Paradox in *Defending Genesis*, namely the idea that the universe is a grand computer simulation. Simulation Theory would have it that the conditions for alien life are right and should be there by all rights but they haven't been plugged into the simulation. Of course, this is purest speculation and actually leaves open the possibility that God is the Grand Programmer, so most materialist prefer to appeal to a similar version of the Multiverse Hypothesis.

The Multiverse is the idea that our Earth is just one of an infinite number of universes, each having a slightly different set of properties. Television shows like Sliders gave us a basic idea of how the concept works, but it's so much more. Princeton cosmologist Paul Steinhardt complained that it is quite literally the Theory of Anything:

And I do mean *anything*. In the Multiverse, there are universes where life doesn't even exist on Earth and where it's as ubiquitous as the Star Wars universe. In the Multiverse, there are universes where you are the President, where you're the opposite gender, and where you're the darkest part of yourself, like that Star Trek episode where Spock had a beard. In the Multiverse, Hitler never existed, lived as a slave during the Civil War, and won and lost a thousand World War I I in a zillion different ways, including getting punched in the nose by Captain America. In the Multiverse, there is an America where the turkey became the national bird and we eat Thanksgiving fish thrice a year. I could go on. All that's required is imagination.

One of the reasons for the Multiverse theory is to get past the Anthropic Principle, the observation that the properties of the universe we inhabit seem finely tuned for life here on Earth. It's a big problem for folks who've hitched their star to pure naturalism because the Anthropic Principle implies a Creator, the ultimate negation of pure naturalism. The Multiverse converts the Anthropic Principle to a weak form; that is, the universe appears to be fine-tuned for life on Earth because we just happen to exist one possible universe with these properties out of a random infinite number of possible universes. As noted, it's also used to sidestep the Fermi Paradox, the observation that the Copernican Principle would predict that life would be common in the universe but, as yet, we appear to be alone. An appeal to the Multiverse washes the paradox away, in theory: we just happen to be in the universe where life should be theoretically ubiquitous but actually only exists here.

Scientifically speaking, the Multiverse is void for vagueness. Steinhardt used the 2014 annual Edge Foundation Question[5] to voice his criticism:

> "A pervasive idea in fundamental physics and cosmology that should be retired: the notion that we live in a multiverse in which the laws of physics and the properties of the cosmos vary randomly from one patch of space to another. According to this view, the laws and properties within our observable universe cannot be

explained or predicted because they are set by chance. Different regions of space too distant to ever be observed have different laws and properties, according to this picture. Over the entire multiverse, there are infinitely many distinct patches. Among these patches, in the words of Alan Guth, "anything that can happen will happen—and it will happen infinitely many times". Hence, I refer to this concept as a Theory of Anything.

Any observation or combination of observations is consistent with a Theory of Anything. No observation or combination of observations can disprove it. Proponents seem to revel in the fact that the Theory cannot be falsified. The rest of the scientific community should be up in arms since an unfalsifiable idea lies beyond the bounds of normal science. Yet, except for a few voices, there has been surprising complacency and, in some cases, grudging acceptance of a Theory of Anything as a logical possibility. The scientific journals are full of papers treating the Theory of Anything seriously.

What is going on?"

In other words, it's just bad science. It can't be falsified and makes no tangible predictions. It's a cop-out that amounts to a shoulder-shrugging pseudoscientific, "Well, that's just the way it is."

When I say there's no way to prove it, I do so with a high level of confidence. You see, our observable samples size of universes is exactly one. Even in theory, we could not observe other universes in the Multiverse. We could speculate that features of our observable universe are evidence of contact with another, but honestly how would we objectively be able to determine whether those features weren't just properties of our lone universe and had nothing to do with the proposed Multiverse?

Now I happen to think the strong Anthropic Principle is evident because our Creator intended to give us, as Blaise Pascal put it, too little evidence to be sure but too much to ignore. I also happen to think that the answer to the Fermi Paradox is that the Copernican Principle is arrogant in its presumption of a purely material universe. Aliens that are kind of rare rather than ubiquitous would cast doubt on a purely naturalistic universe. Of course, the materialist could appeal to the Multiverse and claim that aliens just happen to be rare in this universe when they could be more commonplace. Meanwhile, the creationist could observe that Creator chose to paint on more than one canvas.

One of the intriguing thing about the Multiverse for a sci-fi writer is that it that, in a way, it does exist. It simply exists in imagination and in literature. The worlds we create, especially when we write or film speculative fiction, can be just as real as the one we live and breathe in. You recall that Tolkien likened storytelling to an act of sub-creation, which he further saw as an act of worship. We are made in the image of the Creator; what greater act of worship can there be than creation? Similarly, it may also be that the Multiverse exists as all possible worlds in the mind of God, but again it seems there is no place where the Multiverse exists outside of the realm of imagination.

If we discovered extraterrestrial life at all, it would likely be because said life came calling. I can't imagine that being a good thing. Stephen Hawking has likewise noted that aliens who visit this planet are not likely to be friendly. In fact, he's on record as saying:

> "If aliens ever visit us, I think the outcome would be much as when Christopher Columbus first landed in America, which didn't turn out very well for the Native Americans.[6]"

In all likelihood, they would be planet plundering locusts, hopping from one resource rich world to another. While the universe is full of water and minerals, Earth offers one resource we haven't yet seen anywhere else: protein and chlorophyll, found only in plants and animals. In other words: food and potential biofuel. That is to say, meeting aliens is most likely to look like *Independence Day* than *E.T.*

If they have superior technology to allow themselves to travel across the universe at near light speed without their ships being torn to shreds in the process, then they have really, really good shields and there's not a thing we'd be able to do to said ships with the armaments Earth currently possesses... including the nuclear option! We could hope for a *War of the Worlds* ending, where viruses kill off the aliens, but history shows that the invaded area is usually more affected by the invaders' diseases than the other way 'round! Our truest hope might be that there aren't any aliens at all, merely alien technology sent into the void much as we've sent robots and machines in advance of biological subjects.

Kenneth Forgan has noted that Hawking's prediction is based on three untestable assumptions[7]: ""one– Aliens that explore the Galaxy in person do so because of their aggressive nature, or two– Intelligent beings only evolve from predators or naturally aggressive creatures, or three– Peaceful aliens do not explore the Galaxy." In a Christian worldview, what Hawking would be suggesting is that only Fallen aliens explore the galaxy. Which brings up possible answers to the Fermi Paradox that are unique to Christendom. Maybe the Zoo Hypothesis is correct but the Galactic Clique in Unfallen and therefore unwilling to contact us, an idea reminiscent of the premise of CS Lewis' Space

Trilogy. Or perhaps Hawking is correct in a way in that our yearning for space travel is reflective of our Fallen state. Might it be that on Unfallen worlds, the inhabitants take care of their planets and do not irresponsibly exploit their God-given resources? Perhaps they are then content to explore the world God has given them. Or perhaps they received no command to subdue their world they are content to live in a near-Edenic state. Yes, they live in a Fallen universe, but what if their world is a Garden of sorts, an exception to the rule. We have to admit that even in a world where death and suffering exists, an Unfallen world opens up the possibility that we've unselfishly pooled our resources and knowledge to eliminate most diseases and minimize suffering, the very concept we have in mind when we think of Heaven on Earth.

Biblical Christians take all of these considerations into account and then correctly note that alien life is highly improbable and that, thus far, Earth is the only planet we know of that has life. The trouble is that Christians, especially creationists, have come up with a further argument that the Scriptures *demand* an absence of alien life as a proof of the specialness of earth. In this argument, the creation worldview and the evolutionary worldview are pitted against each other in the form of no alien life as prediction of special creation versus alien life as a prediction of the evolutionary model. For some folks, the issue of creation versus evolution has become so polarized that the very fact that aliens are espoused by evolutionists is reason enough to compel them to oppose it.

Historically speaking, the Church's position on extraterrestrials has almost always been reactionary. The Greek atomists were the first on record to discuss the possibility of extraterrestrial life. Originally proposed by Leucippus (fifth century BC), atomism was developed and refined by his protégé, the "laughing philosopher," Democritus (460-370 BC), called the "father of modern science" by some. The atomists believed that the universe was made up of building blocks called atoms which had randomly assorted themselves to form everything we see. Although materialist, it was an essentially deist position; God started things perhaps but had little to do since then and didn't bother to meddle with the affairs of men at any rate.

Epicurus succeeded Democritus. In a letter to his student Herodotus, he wrote:

> "There are infinite worlds both like and unlike this world of ours. For the atoms being infinite in number…are borne far out into space.[8]"

> "Furthermore, we must believe that in all worlds there are living creatures and plants and other things we see in this world.[9]"

The materialism of atomism developed into atheistic Epicureanism, though Epicurus himself was a deist.

The Roman poet Titus Lucretius Carus (99–55 BC), better known as Lucretius, popularized the Epicurean system of belief, complete with alien worlds, a few decades prior to the birth of Christ.

Now, if we were considering the timing of this popularization of a worldview that was practically identical to modern atheistic evolutionism, we might find it significant that it happened so close to the Incarnation.

In any case, the atomists were opposed by Plato and Aristotle. Both camps believed that the Earth was built from four elements (earth, wind, fire and water), but the atomists believed that outer space was likewise built from these elements, while the Aristotelians believed that space was made from a separate element called ether. Thus, the atomists believed that extraterrestrial life was possible and likely commonplace on a proposed plurality of worlds because it was made from the same elements as Earth. The other camp's beliefs flowed well with geocentrism, both of which were thought to affirm the specialness of Earth. Thus, the Aristotelians believed that, of course, life was special to Earth.

The Church threw in its lot with the Aristotelians because the Epicurean system was atheistic and denied special creation and the specialness of Earth. Epicureanism also denied the idea of an immortal, immaterial soul and an afterlife. Augustine of Hippo (354–430 CE), Albertus Magnus (1193–1280), and Thomas Aquinas (c. 1225–1274) all opposed the idea of extraterrestrial life and the plurality of worlds.

Shortly after, Etienne Tempier, the bishop of Paris, became concerned that theologians were making claims that limited God's power and free will. Article 34 of his famous Condemnation of 1277, condemned the Aristotelian position "that the First Cause [God}] cannot make more than one world." This was meant as a defense against any claim that seemed to restrict God's power, not as an affirmation of the plurality of worlds; however, the net result was that Christians were now free to speculate on the subject and on the existence of extraterrestrial life.

According to patristics scholar Joseph Lienhard[10], the only extraterrestrials the early Christians conceived of were celestial beings or minds who were thought to indwell the sun, moon, and the five visible planets, which accounted for the "rational origin" of their circular motion. For example, in 1440 Nicholas of Cusa (1401–1464) published *Of Learned Ignorance*, wherein he advocated the possibility of extraterrestrial life on the moon and sun.

The theological implications of extraterrestrial life were first considered by William Vorilong (1392-1463) in his commentary of the *Sentences* of Peter Lombard. His assessment was positive.

> "Infinite worlds, more perfect than this one, lie hid in the mind of God. ... It is possible that the species of each of these worlds is

distinguished from those of our world."

It should be said that he did not think we would ever encounter the inhabitants of this world. In fact, he believed that we would only truly know of their existence through supernatural revelation (i.e., angelic messengers, etc.)

As to whether these extraterrestrials would automatically be imputed with an Adamic sin nature, he wrote:

> "If it be inquired whether people, existing on that world, have sinned as Adam sinned, I answer, No. They would not have contracted sin just as their humanity is not from Adam."

It was therefore logical that he did not think Christ would have to be incarnated and sacrificed on a plurality of alien worlds, being unnecessary. Furthermore, he saw Christ's terrestrial sacrifice as sufficient for all organisms in the universe, if their redemption was required it:

> "As to the question whether Christ by dying on this earth could redeem the inhabitants of another world, I answer that he was able to do this not only for our world but for infinite worlds. But it would not be fitting for him to go to

another world to die again."

The rediscovery of the work of the atomists and Epicureans and the rise of Copernican [heliocentric] cosmology created a new crisis in the Church. Combined, these new developments threatened to undermine the idea of special creation and the specialness of Earth. To complicate things, during the Renaissance the doctrine known as the principle of plenitude, wherein theologians that God's omnipotence would require Him to bring into being all that was possible, became popular. This is an extraBiblical idea was first proposed by Plato and Aristotle and then incorporated into the Church's theology through Augustine of Hippo and St. Anselm. It was also adopted by the atomists and Epicureans. The principle of plenitude actually codified the error that Bishop Etienne Tempier was trying to prevent the Condemnation of 1277.

During the Reformation, the principle of plenitude was questioned and opposed, but so was Copernican cosmology. Philip Melanchthon was worried that Copernican cosmology and the principle of plenitude would eventually cause some to conclude that Christ must be born and put to death on multiple worlds. In his 1550 *Initia Doctrinae Physicae*, he wrote:

> "[T]he Son of God is One;...Jesus Christ was born, died, and resurrected in this world. Nor does he manifest Himself elsewhere, nor elsewhere has He died or

resurrected. Therefore it must not be imagined that Christ died and was resurrected more often, nor must it be thought that in any other world without the knowledge of the Son of God, that men would be restored to eternal life."

In other words, he essentially agreed with Vorilong's assessment: if anybody needs salvation besides mankind Christ died once for the universe, right here on Earth.

To be fair, Giordano Bruno enthusiastically espoused the idea of extraterrestrial life alongside a multitude of actual heresies, including a denial of eternal damnation, the Trinity, the divinity of Christ, the virginity of Mary, and transubstantiation. He was burned at the stake in Rome's Campo de' Fiori at the hands of the Inquisition in 1600.

Copernican cosmology eventually gained traction. The Church had espoused geocentrism because it was part of the Aristotelean tradition which opposed Epicureanism and because it seemed to mesh well with the anthropocentric emphasis of the Bible. If the Earth was the center of God's attention, why should it also not be the center of the universe He created?

There is a lesson here. Categorizing the idea that "alien life does not exist" as a prediction of special creation is the worst sort of overstatement, precisely because we are in real danger of setting up a Galileo debacle here. In Galileo's day, folks had found proof texts in the Bible that could be seen as supporting the geocentric Ptolemaic/Aristotelian cosmological model. One of the major arguments for geocentrism was the idea that the Earth was special in God's sight. Now we know that we are neither the center of our solar system nor the center of the universe, except from a relative perspective. Our physical place in the universe makes us no less exceptional in God's sight.

Theological Geocentrism

A lot of Christians posit a sort of theological geocentrism; that is, we think of the Earth as the center of the universe with all the rest of the universe as mere background. One of the primary passages anti-alienists use to back up this idea is Isaiah 45:18. For example, Dr. Danny Faulkner wrote the following in an article entitled "Is Belief in Alien Life Harmless?" in the Oct/Dec 2015 issue of *Answers* magazine:

> "Isaiah 45:18 makes a distinction between God's role for the earth and the heavens (the rest of the universe). It says that God did not create the earth in vain, but that He made it to be inhabited. While the Bible is not geocentric (placing the earth at the physical center of the universe), the earth is the center of God's attention. Humans—and not ETs—are God's primary concern in the universe."

Christians believe that the Earth is special and that God is actively involved in the affairs of its inhabitants. It may be true that the Earth is the center of God's attention. He did created mankind in His own image after all. I won't argue with that.

I can and will argue with the idea that just because Scripture says that God did not create the Earth in vain (empty) that this is meant as an iron-clad contrast with the heavens. We have three statements: God created the heavens. God created the earth. God did not create it in vain but to be inhabited. This does not necessarily imply that He by contrast made the heavens in vain to be uninhabited. Yet we have creationist organizations making absurd statements like this one made in Chapter 18 of the *New Answers Book*:

> "But where does the Bible discuss the creation of life on the "lights in the expanse of the heavens"? There is no such description because the lights in the expanse were not designed to accommodate life."

That, my friends, is a *bona fide* argument from silence, the weakest and most inadvisable of all arguments. The Bible is equally silent about microbes and Black holes. We cannot say that the heavens were not designed for life simply because the Bible fails to mention this as being the case. It may simply be that the Bible's revelation is, well, geocentric and does not concern itself with the affairs of God's creations "in a galaxy far, far away." It is certainly true that from an Earthbound perspective, the stars provide light and signs for season and a sense of awe at God's creative power, but it may be that the Bible does not mention any other purpose for the heavens simply because it doesn't concern us. The Bible's silence regarding extraterrestrial lifeforms would not invalidate its inerrancy. We might simply note that extraterrestrial life was not really germane to the discussion as it were.

The context of Isaiah 45:18 is that God is assuring Israel that He is in control and that there is a purpose to everything He's doing; there is a plan. God here is saying nothing more than He did just a few short verses before when He declared:

> "I have made the earth, and created man upon it: I, *even* my hands, have stretched out the heavens, and all their host have I commanded."

In Isaiah 45:18, God is saying, "I created the heavens. I created the Earth. I created the Earth with every intention of creating man. I had a plan when I created the universe, just as I have a plan for Israel and I did not make my promises to Jacob in vain." To say that Isaiah 45:18 precludes the possibility of alien life is simply overstatement, because in order to do so one has to force a contrast that doesn't really exist in the text. The text does say that God created the earth to be inhabited; it does not say He created the heavens to be uninhabited.

Gambling Against the Improbable

My fear now is that is that creationist will have erroneously canonized this idea that our position, the Biblical position, predicts an absence of alien life. It is a great leap from strong suggestion to actual prediction. We need to refrain from such dogmatism where we cannot yet be certain in the absence of a clear Scriptural revelation. Inference isn't quite enough in these cases.

If life is common in the universe, we've certainly seen no evidence of it. The Fermi Paradox asks, "If the universe is teeming with life, where is everybody?" The Star Wars universe, the Star Trek universe, the Marvel Cinematic Universe and similar fictional worlds where the ether simply teems with alien civilizations are based on an evolutionary worldview.

Well, sort of.

If we're fair about it, we have to ask ourselves why most of these fictional aliens can interbreed with us with fertile offspring. Because that makes biological sense, right? Just about as much sense as various worlds independently developing humanoid intelligent life that looks pretty much like us in the first place, huh? Science fictions aside, there's no way to know whether life is rare or abundant in the universe.

If life is common in the universe, there's no reason to conclude it's just as probable there is no God.

After all, abiogenesis and molecules-to-man evolution are so statistically improbable as to rate impossibility. Multiplying zero by infinity doesn't really add up to better odds. I tend to think if the all-natural Just-so story they've concocted were true, they've used up all of their odds on Earth alone and the chances of it happening again become less likely not as likely or more likely. In other words, if life were common in the universe, this invokes the supernatural, for it proposes that nature must overcome do impossible things. It actually makes it more probable that God does exist!

One of the strongest objections among Bible-believing Christians to the idea of extraterrestrial life is that it is an idea rooted in evolution. Certainly, the idea that alien life exists elsewhere in the universe is consistent with the naturalistic worldview; however, it's not inconsistent with the Biblical Christian worldview either.

It should come as little surprise that conservative Christianity's current anti-alien stance is mostly a reaction against the rise of Darwinian biology. In the minds of many, Christianity's special place in both astronomy and biology had been rudely displaced, casting further doubt on the faith once delivered. Most Creationists recognize that all-natural microbes-to-man evolution has its root in the atomist/Epicurean systems and their rediscovery, particularly in the writings of Lucretius.

During the Enlightenment, the principle of plenitude provided a justification for the plurality of worlds;

that is, people assumed that God would not waste space by leaving planets lifeless. If it's not obvious by now, the principle of plentitude's major flaw is that while God can do anything He pleases that is consistent with His revealed character and attributes, He's not truly omnipotent unless He can choose not to do absolutely everything He's capable of.

In 1793, Thomas Paine argued in the Age of Reason that given the scale of the universe and the plurality of worlds contained in it, the Earth was very insignificant:

> "Alas! what is this [Earth] to the mighty ocean of space, and the almighty power of the Creator?
>
> From whence, then, could arise the solitary and strange conceit that the Almighty, who had millions of worlds equally dependent on his protection, should quit the care of all the rest, and come to die in our world, because, they say, one man and one woman had eaten an apple? And, on the other hand, are we to suppose that every world in the boundless creation had an Eve, an apple, a serpent, and a redeemer? In this case, the person who is irreverently called the Son of God, and sometimes God himself, would have nothing else

to do than to travel from world to world, in an endless succession of deaths, with scarcely a momentary interval of life."

This pseudo-theological objection continues today, despite the fact that men such as William Vorilong and Philip Melanchthon argued that since these aliens did not spring from Adam, multiple Incarnations are unnecessary. Alas! Christianity was already battening down the hatches against a storm of opposition during the Enlightenment and, once again, the Church's position was a mere reaction to its critics' position. Once the idea of extraterrestrial life became linked to Darwinism and the related idea of panspermia, the conservative Church became increasingly opposed to the ET hypothesis.

Of course, we shouldn't base our beliefs on mere contradiction to those who oppose us.

***

Notes

1. Morrison, David. Ask an Astrobiologist. NASA.gov.Senior Scientist at the NASA (July 10, 2006). Quoted from Web Archive: https://web.archive.org/web/20060928234811/http://nai.arc.nasa.gov/astrobio/astrobio_detail.cfm?ID=1551. Retrieved October 18, 2016.

2. Weintraub, David A. *Religions and Extraterrestrial Life: How Will We Deal With*

It? Springer Praxis Book (2014), p. 5.

3. As quoted in Gates, Sara. "We Are Not Alone In the Universe, NASA Scientists Say." HuffingtonPost.com. (July 15, 2014). Web. Retrieved October 18, 2016.

4. Crick, Francis. Life Itself: Its Origin and Nature. Simon & Schuster (1981), p.88.

5. Steinhardt, Paul. "Theories of Anything." WHAT SCIENTIFIC IDEA IS READY FOR RETIREMENT? edge.org (March 9, 2014). Retrieved November 23, 2016

6. As quoted in "Episode 1: Aliens." *Into the Universe with Stephen Hawking.* Discovery Channel. Television. (April 25, 2010).

7. Bonner, Walt. "Are Aliens Avoiding Earth?" FoxNews.com (September 23, 2016). Web.

8. Epicurus, "Letter to Herodotus," translated by Cyril Bailey in *The Stoic and Epicurean Philosophers*, ed. Whitney J. Oates. Random House (1940), p. 5.

9. Ibid., p. 13.

10. Wiker, Benjamin. "Alien Ideas: Christianity and the Search for Extraterrestrial Life." CrisisMagazine.com. (June 27, 2009). Web. Retrieved October 18, 2016.

Tony Breeden

13 Angels and Aliens

I mentioned in a previous chapter that Ancient Astronaut advocates tend to mention the Nephilim of Genesis 6, insinuating that "sons of God" who procreated with humans to produce these mighty men of renown were actually aliens. The meaning of this passage is disputed, but it does appear that the plain meaning of the text is that fallen angels (presumably those who "left their first estate, but left their own habitation" [Jude 1:6]) procreated with human women, resulting in a race of giants[1]. Certainly, the fallen angel view is the earliest position on the passage and makes the most sense.

Nevertheless, there is some disagreement as to whether the "sons of God" of Genesis 6 were men or angels, and there is no disputing that Ezekiel's Wheel is associated with angels. Aliens aren't really mentioned in Scripture. Some folks will claim that since the Bible is silent on life beyond this planet and since extraterrestrial life is an evolutionary concept in their minds, there's no such thing as extraterrestrial life. This is the sort of baseless dogma that has shot Christendom in the pants in the past. If the Bible is silent about a subject, it does not automatically follow that it must not exist. An argument from silence is one of the weakest of all possible arguments. If it does exist and we have not considered that possibility, many will feel that our worldview has been invalidated because a few boneheads decided it was impossible based on the fact that the Bible made it highly improbable, but not impossible after all.

In the last chapter, we mentioned the erroneous assumption that extraterrestrial life would confirm the evolutionary worldview. The evolutionary worldview does come with the assumption that life on other planets must be pretty common and that it developed by purely natural means.

By contrast, the Bible declares that God specially created life in the universe:

> "For by him all things were created, in heaven and on earth, visible and invisible, whether thrones or dominions or rulers or authorities—all things were created through him and for him." Colossians 1:16.

God made everything. He made plants. Animals. Microbes. Angelic beings. Mankind. And if they exist, He made aliens.

As Jill Tarter[2], director of the Center for SETI Research notes:

> "If God exists and extraterrestrials exist, God was responsible for them, so how can their existence undermine God?"

Some have objected that extraterrestrials could not exist because they do not see how aliens could fit into God's greater purpose. This is essentially an argument from personal incredulity. "How would ETs fit into God's greater purpose?" is an amazing question. It's probably unanswerable because, well, God's thoughts are higher than ours and, frankly, we don't have enough information. What is the purpose of all the stars and infinite worlds that are only detectable by telescopes as powerful as Hubble if they were solely meant to serve mankind by being objects to light the night sky, to mark off seasons [Genesis 1:14-19]? One might here object that such far flung heavenly bodies fulfill the revealed purpose of proclaiming the omnipotence and majesty of God [Psalm 19:1], but I can't help but feel we're being reductionist by stating that these revealed stated purposes of heavenly bodies necessarily implies that there are no unstated purposes to said bodies. Furthermore, even if I do not know how ETs fit into God's greater purpose, I can assure you that if they do in fact exist, they do fit into God's greater purpose somehow.

The fact of the matter is that the Bible is not silent on the matter of the existence of extraterrestrial sapient beings. Angels were created some time before man. Scripture reveals that there are different forms of angels: seraphim, cherubim, archangels, living creatures that seem to be amalgams of Earth creatures... and some of them are quite bizarre. They recognize that they are not the Creator God; for example, the angel who speaks to John in Revelation tells him not to bow before him because they are both equally servants of God. Spiritually speaking, some are fallen and some are not, definitely suggesting free will on their part.

The very Biblical fact of angels (fallen or otherwise) in God's court implies that Earth may not be unique, except possibly where it concerns beings created in His image. Of course, it's probably better to say angel when we mean angel and alien when we mean alien because folks have very, very different images in their heads of what those terms mean. Generally speaking, men are not inferring biological extraterrestrial organisms indigenous to another planet when they speak of angels.

In His Image

Another objection commonly brought up by Christians to the idea of extraterrestrial life is the argument that only man was made in the image of God. For the record, I'm not arguing against that. The Bible says that man was created in God's image and I believe that. The trouble is that a lot of Christian theologians have declared that the meaning of being made in God's image is that we have a mind, ruling out any other sapient creations in the universe.

In their defense, it's not really clear what is meant by this particular phrase. Scripture never bothers to clarify the matter, so we've had to infer its meaning. It's obvious that we are not God's image-bearers in terms of physicality because the Bible says that God is a spirit [John 4:24]. So we're left to figure out what that means by contrasting ourselves with other life forms; we came up with intelligence, communication, immortality, a spiritual aspect, creativity, love, freedom, morality and a whole host of other attributes that seemed to have one thing in common – we have a mind.

Unfortunately, while we were busy contrasting ourselves with beasts, we forgot that the angelic beings, as revealed in Scripture, have all of these same attributes. Colossians 1:16 makes it pretty clear that if something exists, God created it, and that would include the angels.

Either intelligence and a spiritual aspect is not what is meant by being made in the image of God, or else the angels were also made in God's image. The Scripture explicitly says that man was created in God's image; it doesn't say that God never made anything else in His image. Of course, we have no Scriptural revelation one way or the other as to whether angels were or weren't made in God's image, so the whole matter is purest speculation. Yet we cannot deny that when they walk among us, they look human enough. In Bible, angels speak, eat, sing, and even wrestle with folks like Jacob. If the passages about the Nephilim and the angels fallen from their first estate refer to fallen angels interbreeding in a physical form with human women, they're a lot more like us than we generally acknowledge. At the very least, we could say that they have the power to become human, or else such interbreeding would not be possible at all!

While we cannot rule out that angels are not made in

God's image, I do not think this is the case, precisely because God has dealt with fallen mankind and angels so differently. The lengths that God went to in order to graciously provide a means of salvation for man, when no such remedy is evident for angels, suggests that there really is something special about man... and I believe that is that we were made in God's image and the angels were not.

On the other hand, we don't really know when angels were made. Since in the beginning God made everything in heaven and earth in six calendar days about 6,000 years ago, we presume that angels were made during the Creation Week. We further postulate that the fall of angels occurred previously to the Fall of Man a relatively short time after their creation because a fallen angel (Satan) tempted Eve in the Garden. These are inferences. Literary apologist JC Lamont took a different approach in her *Chronicles of Time* series. In that series, angels were part of God's creative efforts before the beginning of this universe. In other words, she speculated about the idea that the phrase, "In the beginning," simply means the beginning of the universe and that God, being an eternally existent Creator, might not have limited His efforts to this universe alone.

The interesting thing about that hypothesis is that it might explain a few mysteries. It might explain why God doesn't explicitly mention the creation of the angels, the four living creatures and other creatures we find mentioned in association with angels, fallen or otherwise. If intelligence and a spiritual aspect are what is meant by being made in God's image, then the angels would qualify. It's an intriguing concept to speculate that angels are beings who were created in another universe that exist before ours. We know that they are fellow servants with humanity. Did they fall and find redemption in the Son sent to their world? We know that if Christians are saved and somehow fell from grace that no other sacrifice would be available for them. Is it possible that the reason that angels and men are treated so differently where it concerns salvation is because the angels who fell with Satan were once upon a time redeemed from a previously fallen state and now no further sacrifice is available for their redemption, as God sent His Son to their universe to die once for all for their inhabitants?

I write speculative fiction, so I am practiced at exploring such possibilities. I am also quite adept at spotting plot holes. One of the things that stands out to me is that the Bible says we shall judge angels. Why would that be necessary if a Redeemer had ever been sent to them? More to the point, if man has been given the Dominion Mandate, wouldn't that only apply to the heavens and earth of this universe? How would we then judge inhabitants of a different universe?

The Dominion Mandate

For those of you unfamiliar with the Dominion Mandate, I'm referring to Genesis 1:26-28:

> 26 And God said, Let us make

man in our image, after our likeness: and let them have dominion over the fish of the sea, and over the fowl of the air, and over the cattle, and over all the earth, and over every creeping thing that creepeth upon the earth.

27 So God created man in his own image, in the image of God created he him; male and female created he them.

28 And God blessed them, and God said unto them, Be fruitful, and multiply, and replenish the earth, and subdue it: and have dominion over the fish of the sea, and over the fowl of the air, and over every living thing that moveth upon the earth.

These verses state that man was created to have dominion over the earth and the creatures of the earth. One should note that this dominion would be exercised under the sovereignty of God, who bestowed this dominion to man. The Dominion Mandate is important to this discussion because folks such as Gary Bates claim that if we encounter intelligent ETs it would be a violation of the Dominion Mandate. He proposes that any extraterrestrials we encounter with the ability to reach Earth must needs be more technologically advanced and therefore, whether friendly or otherwise, they would end up having dominion over mankind in direct contradiction of Scripture.

At first glance, the Dominion Mandate seems only to apply man's dominion to the Earth and the creatures that inhabit it; however Strong's Lexicon Hebrew notes that the word rendered "air" in verses 26 and 28 is *shaw-mah'-yim* (8064), "a dual of an unused singular *shameh* {*shaw-meh'*}; from an unused root meaning to be lofty; the sky (as aloft; the dual perhaps alluding to the visible arch in which the clouds move, as well as to the higher ether where the celestial bodies revolve)."

If that's the case, this passage could refer to both the First and Second Heavens as being part of the dominion of man, and this seems likely given the universal effect of the Fall; in other words, it would explain why all of the cosmos was subjected to futility as a result of man's sin and not merely the Earth [Romans 8:18-22; Colossians 1:20].

Some see the Dominion Mandate as a command to have dominion over the Earth, but this is not something we get from the original Hebrew. Rather the impression we get is that God bestowed dominion upon man as a position of appointment. Worse still for those clinging to the idea that the Dominion Mandate theologically prevents the existence of intelligent extraterrestrial life, the Dominion Mandate may now have passed from man.

Darek Isaacs[3], writing in the *Answers Research Journal*, noted that man evidences no dominion over either the Earth nor the animals, despite the Dominion Mandate being repeated to Noah post-Flood. We may domesticate animals, but it is nothing like the picture of dominion painted for the restored future creation, which creationists believe is a return to the Edenic state. As he pointedly reminds us, rather than a child leading a calf and lion together in dominion, in today's world, the lion would exercise a horrible dominion over both the calf and the child! Essentially, Adam's dominion is broken, when he chose autonomy from God by disobeying God's command and put himself under Satan's dominion. God retains the ultimate right, but Satan has presently made his throne on Earth. Isaacs then convincingly argues that Messiah now has the dominion, as evidenced by the forty disciples having power not only over demons but over animals (in being able to tread upon scorpions and serpents). When one is born again, they are transferred from the dominion of darkness to the dominion of Christ and may by faith exercise dominion through Him.

If this is the case, and I strongly believe it is, then the Dominion Mandate has no bearing on the question of extraterrestrials. If intelligent aliens exist, they cannot be said to be infringing upon the Adamic Dominion Mandate if this dominion has passed from the First Adam to the Last Adam. Even if mankind fell under an extraterrestrial race's dominion, it would not mean Christ's dominion was infringed upon, any more than being under the persecution of the Roman Empire here on Earth infringed upon the dominion of Christ.

Some have tried to wed the Dominion Mandate to what it means to be made in the image of God. Since it is still unclear what the image of God actually means, it is equally unclear whether this is warranted. Whatever the phrase means, it seems to be clear to God alone. Perhaps it was more evident before we were fallen. If the Dominion Mandate is synonymous with the image of God and Isaacs is correct about the Dominion Mandate, it would mean that mankind no longer reflects the image of God; after all, 2 Corinthians 3:18 says:

> "But we all, with open face
> beholding as in a glass the glory of
> the Lord, are changed into the
> same image from glory to glory,
> even as by the Spirit of the Lord."

Perhaps this speaks of a progressive restoration into the image of God. And the Bible does say that Christ will restore all things unto Himself [Colossians 1:20].

We still note that the Dominion Mandate given to Adam would not have included dominion over anything beyond the heavens and the earth of this cosmos. Given that boundary, we need to determine whether it is possible to determine when angels were created.

Job 38:4–7 says:

> "Where were you when I laid the
> foundations of the earth? Tell Me,

if you have understanding. Who determined its measurements? Surely you know! Or who stretched the line upon it? To what were its foundations fastened? Or who laid its cornerstone, When the morning stars sang together, and all the sons of God shouted for joy?

So angels, called "sons of God" and the "morning stars" in verse 7, "shouted for joy" when God created the heavens and the Earth, specifically when He laid the foundations of the earth. So this is either a reference to Day 1, when God made the heavens and the earth, or Day 3 when He made the dry land.

Possible support for the idea that angels were created during the Creation Week comes Ezekiel 28:13–15:

> You were in Eden, the garden of God; every precious stone was your covering: the sardius, topaz, and diamond, beryl, onyx, and jasper, sapphire, turquoise, and emerald with gold. The workmanship of your timbrels and pipes was prepared for you on the day you were created. You were the anointed cherub who covers; I established you; you were on the holy mountain of God; you walked back and forth in the midst of fiery stones. You were perfect in your

ways from the day you were created, till iniquity was found in you.

If the "day you were created" refers to an actual day, we could point out that time itself began on Day 1. Of course, it could also be a figure of speech like the non-literal day found in Genesis 2:4. Further support is found in Psalm 104:1-5:

> 1 Bless the LORD, O my soul. O LORD my God, thou art very great; thou art clothed with honour and majesty.
>
> 2 Who coverest thyself with light as with a garment: who stretchest out the heavens like a curtain:
>
> 3 Who layeth the beams of his chambers in the waters: who maketh the clouds his chariot: who walketh upon the wings of the wind:
>
> 4 Who maketh his angels spirits; his ministers a flaming fire:
>
> 5 Who laid the foundations of the earth, that it should not be removed for ever.

Genesis tells us that God created the heavens and the earth, as well as light, on Day 1 of the Creation Week. On Day 3, He molded the earth He fashioned on that First day. In Psalm 104, we find a reference to God making light and then, sandwiched between a description of God stretching out the heavens and laying the foundations of the earth, we find a reference to angels in verse 4. I don't believe this is an accident. I believe angels were brought into existence at the very beginning of the Creation Week when God stretched out the cosmos and brought light upon the formless earth.

What does it matter when angels were created and where? Well, it matters a lot where it concerns our argument for the possibility of extraterrestrial life. If the angels were created on Day 1 or 2, but in time to observe God in action on Day 3, it means that they are part of the heavens and earth which given to Adam as part of the original Dominion Mandate. It means that they are immortal (not eternal; only God who has neither beginning nor end is eternal) despite being intelligent, volitional beings with a spiritual aspect who are subject to the universal effects of the Fall. If this were the case, we would have to ask ourselves why angels do not die when everything else we see here on earth does not. It is not a matter of being unfallen, for even fallen angels are apparently immortal. What if angels do not die because they were not cursed with the sanguine effects of the Fall that only apply to Adam's bloodline. If we read the account of the Fall of man in Genesis 3 carefully, we note that the ground, plants and animals were cursed. Man was certainly cursed. What about the angels? If angels qualify as image bearers by dint of being intelligent, volitional beings with a spiritual aspect, were image-bearers exempt because volitional beings must fall on their own merits? Perhaps.

Some may object that angels belong to heaven [Jude 1:6], the realm of God which is beyond this material universe. As such, they argue, angels exist beyond time and universe and all that, which makes them exempt from the effects of the Curse. It may be true that being citizens of the Third heaven, or heaven of heavens, may exempt angels from death and all the other effects of the Fall of Man, but I object to the idea that they were created outside of time. Angels are immortal, meaning they had a beginning. They were created by God who alone is eternal, having neither beginning nor end. So angels must be subject to time, which is condition of the cosmos God created. Nehemiah 9:6 seems to confirm this:

> You, even you, are LORD alone;
> you have made heaven, the heaven
> of heavens, with all their host, the
> earth, and all things that are
> therein, the seas, and all that is
> therein, and you preserve them all;
> and the host of heaven worships
> you.

Note when it speaks of God making the heavens the parenthetical remark regarding God making the heaven of heavens and all their hosts before going on to mention the earth and the seas. It seems pretty clear that when God made the heavens and the earth on Day 1 of the Creation Week, the creation of

God's Third Heaven was implicit in that act. So angels may be spirit, but they are subject to time so that they had a beginning. There is something distinct about this Third Heaven from the rest of the heavens.

We know from 2 Peter 3:10-13 that the heavens and earth will be consumed with fire [cp. Rev. 6:14; 20:11], but then there shall be a new heaven and earth afterward [cp. Isaiah 65:17; 66:22; Romans 8:21; Revelations 21:1]. How shall the saints escape this great destruction to see the new heavens and earth? The answer we most directly infer is that we will find safety in the abode of God, in the Third Heaven. If this is the case, we must allow that the Third Heaven is exempt from any effects of the Fall of Adam; how else could it be, since sin cannot enter into the presence of God and He makes His abode there?

If the first estate and habitation of the angels [Jude 1:6] is indeed the Third Heaven, then they would be outside the parameters of the Adamic Dominion Mandate and therefore exempt from the effects of the Fall (e.g. death, corruption and depravity). On the other hand, 1 Corinthians 6:3 says that one day the saints will judge angels. The word "judge" here is *krino*, which means "to rule or govern." As joint-heirs with Christ, we will share in His dominion and be in authority over the angels one day. Some may object that angels are under our authority now because Hebrews 1:14 says that angels were created as ministering spirits to help mankind; however, we must note that our authority over angels, fallen or otherwise, comes from Christ's dominion and authority, *not* the Adamic Dominion Mandate, so they appear to be under the saints' authority specifically and not mankind's. This would be consistent with our theory that angels, even if made in the image of God in the sense of having intelligence and a spiritual nature, do not warrant salvation by Christ because they were outside the boundaries of the Fall's effective range.

In any case, since they were likely created during the Creation Week as inhabitants of the Third Heaven, the very fact that angels exist as sapient non-human extraterrestrial life forms disproves the notion that special creation predicts that God did not create life apart from that which exists on Earth. Discounting the Third Heaven as a purely supernatural realm ignores the fact that God created it. In light of this fact, it would seem odd, though not impossible, that God would choose to populate the First and Third Heaven with life, but leave the Second Heaven uninhabited.

We further note that while the existence of angels disproves the notion that special creation predicts that God did not create life apart from that which exists on Earth, their existence does not really clear up whether aliens need to be saved or not; fallen angels fell apart from Adam. They seem neither to require nor warrant salvation, but it is unclear whether this state of affairs is uniquely conditional to their original state or habitation, or whether it has something to do with not being of Adam's bloodline.

***

Notes

1. For an excellent resource on this subject, I recommend Tim Chaffey's book, *The Sons of God and the Nephilim*. CreateSpace Publishing (2011).

2. Kuhn, Robert Lawrence. "Would Intelligent Aliens Undermine God?" ScienceandReligionToday.com. (March 18, 2010), Web.

3. Isaacs, Derek. "Is There A Dominion Mandate?" *Answers Research Journal* (2013), Vol. 6., pp. 1-16.

14 Can Aliens Be Saved?

At the 100 Year Starship Symposium sponsored by DARPA (Defense Advanced Research Projects Agency) in 2011, philosophy professor Christian Weidemann of Germany's Ruhr-University Bochum gave a talk entitled, "Did Jesus Die for Klingons Too?" Weidemann, a self-professed evangelical Christian summed up the problem this way:

> "According to Christianity, an historic event some 2,000 years ago was supposed to save the whole of creation. You can grasp the conflict."

Weidemann discussed the idea that perhaps the aliens didn't need saved, but felt that the principle of mediocrity would suggest that if intelligent life exists somewhere among the stars, they're probably sinners like us. Therefore, he concluded:

> "If there are extraterrestrial intelligent beings at all, it is safe to assume that most of them are sinners too. If so, did Jesus save them too? My position is no. If so, our position among intelligent beings in the universe would be very exceptional."

To be fair, the principle of mediocrity would also argue that, given the existence of life quarantined to a certain extent on Earth, that life typically exists on Earth-like planets throughout the universe. We've not yet been able to determine whether any Earth-like planets have life, so I think this rather overstates the case, as most generalizations do. The real problem with the principle of mediocrity in this case is that it risks committing the mirror image fallacy, the misconception that another group is just a mirror image of ourselves and will therefore react as we would, suffer the same conditions, etc. To be more specific, applying the principle of mediocrity to alien life where it regards depravity (aka Original Sin) begs the question of why they are fallen and also whether intelligence or even dominion is what is meant by being made in God's image.

In this chapter, we will get to the crux of the matter: Would aliens require salvation?

Which brings us to a point any serious Bible student must consider regarding alien life: How did Adam's sin affect other sapient beings in the universe? Are all sapient beings fallen in Adam? Or are there unfallen sentient, moral non-humans who must endure a fallen universe?

Interestingly enough, C.S. Lewis Space Trilogy imagines Earth the "Silent Planet," as a place that is more or less quarantined because we alone are fallen. In doing so, he painted an anti-Wellsian picture of the universe where man was the problem rather than a superior being meant to conquer and reign. Indeed, *Out of the Silent Planet* turns *The War of the Worlds* on its head, with Earthlings invading peaceful Mars, who seem weaker but only because they aren't prone to violence and progress at the expense of others, etc.

In fictional versions of our universe, we get to choose whether aliens are fallen or not, but we need to ask ourselves: Yet what if we did find life on other planets? Would the Bible then be invalid? Can ET be saved?

Just How Alien Are These Aliens?

Before we can ask ourselves whether ET can be saved, I think we need to ask whether he needs to be.

The entire idea that aliens need to be saved is based on the idea that Adam's sin affected the whole cosmos because he was given dominion over all creation. A king falls and his kingdom suffers. So far, so good. We immediately note a difference in the way animals and humans were affected by the Fall. The animals suffered what we might call the universal effects of the Fall (death, suffering, adaptations to the struggle for resources, etc.), but man also inherited a sin nature (what we call depravity). Depravity is like a computer virus that comes with each replicated program. Everyone of Adam's bloodline is affected by it. Christ was required to incarnate as a human in order to be man's kinsman-redeemer, so that His death could free us from the curse of sin and death and His resurrection could give us the promise of eternal life. Again, so far, so good.

The trouble comes when we bring up the possibility of intelligent ETs with a spiritual aspect. It should be noted that we're talking about intelligence at or above the human level here. Ape, insect or dolphin intelligence just don't count.

We should have to first note that non-sapient life would constitute no Biblical challenge. At all. But let's take this one step at a time.

First, we should consider the most likely scenario; namely, that we discover specks of life on some Mars meteor or bacterial life within our own solar system.

It should be said here that the discovery of microbial life in our solar system might not even qualify as purely extraterrestrial in the final analysis. The simplest explanation might well be that such life forms are colonists originally hailing from Earth and that they hitched a ride into space aboard ejecta launched out of our orbit from super-volcanoes or meteorite impacts, such as those we associate with the Noachian Flood.

A meteorite hits the Earth. It divots out a chunk of Earth rock and flings it out of orbit and the amazingly resilient organisms survive the rigors of space and eventually land on other planets or moons in our very own solar system.

Yet what if it weren't from Earth? What if it were methane-based instead of carbon-based? Would that discount the Biblical revelation of special Creation?

One of the more famous episodes of the original Star Trek television series was "Devil in the Dark," in which the crew of the Enterprise encounter a strange subterranean monster in a mining facility on Janus VI. William Shatner stated in his memoirs that this was his favorite episode and it's pretty easy to see why. By the point the Enterprise arrives, the creature has already killed 50 workers and damaged the mine's equipment. After their first encounter, Spock determines that the creature is a silicon-based life form that can burrow through rock via acid secretions. Later in the episode, Spock performs a mind meld and determines that the creature, which calls itself a Horta, is actually intelligent and that all of its actions had been an attempt to protect its eggs. In the end, the human miners and the Horta come to an agreement: the Horta will tunnel where they want, the miners will mine the minerals, and each race will leave the other alone. A pretty surprising outcome for an episode that began with Spock claiming there was no life at all below the planet's surface, "at least, no life as we know it."

The point of the episode is that it may turn out that life on other planets is vastly different than ours. We may not even recognize it as such. Or at the very least, we may not realize it's intelligent.

I digress.

Keep in mind that the question of non-sapient alien life isn't really a threat to anyone's doctrine. They would be subject to this fallen world in much the same way animals and plants and microbes are on this planet. Since Genesis says that God created creatures according to their kind, creationists would expect xenomorphs to be classifiable by kinds.

Oh, I'm sure evolutionists would hail the discovery of extraterrestrial life as a victory for their theory, but that's what they do with every new discovery anyway. Biblicists would simply be forced to recognize that their understanding of the specialness of Earth had nothing to do with the presence of life here, but rather that God created beings in His own image here. Just as we had to adjust our view of the specialness of Earth when geocentrism was disproven.

The problem for Christianity where geocentrism was concerned was not so much that the Bible taught it – there were verses which appeared to coincide with this idea, but which never demanded such a view – but that this science had been erroneously hailed as a truth of the Christian worldview. Interestingly enough, my grandfather told me that there were once preachers who said that man would never reach the moon because God had stopped mankind from building the Tower of Babel. They said that Psalm 115:16 made it clear that man would not be allowed to trespass into the heavens. With all due respect to conspiracy theorists who believe the moon landing was fake, those preachers were wrong. The Bible wasn't wrong, but they misled folks into thinking it was by overstating what it actually said.

Non-sapient life could be as intellectually and socially complex as ants, bees, locusts, dolphins or even apes and still pose no challenge to doctrine. Despite their social complexity, bees are still animals. They do not require salvation. They are fallen with this world, but they have no souls to save! So the extraterrestrials could even be quite socially or intellectually complex, but still not be truly sapient.

Before we move on, I need to address one last thing. I once read a really bad argument that said that if aliens die, it means they are worthy of death. That begs the question of whether animals are worthy of death or if he was just utilizing a double standard to defend his anti-alien stance when he started speaking of intelligent beings affected by Man's Fall. I think it's the latter.

If extraterrestrials aren't intelligent, they're animals. The Bible makes it clear that animals don't need to be saved.

Does ET Have a Soul?

The Bible says that we are made in God's image. A lot of folks think that having a mind and a spiritual aspect is what is meant by being made in God's image; however, if we're fair about it, the angels also meet these qualifications and would also qualify as being made in God's image if this were true. Unless being God's image-bearer means something else entirely, known only to God Himself.

If the extraterrestrial is intelligent but lacks a spiritual aspect... First of all, that would be a critter we've never seen. We may see it in the form of future artificial intelligence. I've often thought that Revelation 13:15 could turn out to be a prophetic reference to artificial intelligence. I dealt with the issues of depravity and artificial intelligence in a short story called "Bad Program." I believe that the problem with artificial intelligence is that it will never be true intelligence, it will merely mimic intelligence. As such, if it begins mimicking the human concern for its robot soul, I think we will have done the poor thing a disservice for by what theory does a robot gain a soul through sufficient complexity of intelligence? If we say yes, we are saying that robots are now made in the image of God rather than in the image of man. If we say no, as we must (given the absurdity of the alternative), we are saying that intelligence alone is not enough to qualify one as being made in God's image.

In any case, if the extraterrestrial lacks a spiritual aspect, an eternal soul to save, then it does not need saving.

Are Intelligent ETs Truly Volitional Beings?

Some believe that morality is one of the things that makes us God's image-bearers. This is likely what leads folks like Gary Bates to protest that it "seems bizarre to assign no moral responsibility for the actions of highly intelligent beings." Of course, we're not suggesting that intelligent ETs have no moral responsibility for their actions; we're just saying that it seems even more bizarre to hold them morally responsible for Adam's sin at all!

We also note that Bates is presuming that intelligent extraterrestrials would be moral agents. Perhaps it's because he can't conceive of such a thing as an amoral intelligent agent, but I can. I said before that aliens could be as intelligent as bees or dolphins with no worries for Christianity. The fact is that ETs could even be vastly more intelligent than that, if they were not moral agents. For example, some computer programs are very intelligent. They can also seem very human; we've even managed to get a few to pass the Turing test, meaning that they have passed for human in a blind test. But programs (and any robots we insert them into) are intelligent but amoral. They do what they're designed to do and they have no other choice. Men and angels made volitional choices that caused their fallen states.

If extraterrestrials are not truly volitional agents, they don't need to be saved.

Are ETs Fallen?

Let's say then that we discover a creature that is intelligent and has a spiritual aspect. Does it follow that these aliens need saving? Well, that depends upon whether it is fallen or not and how it fell.

We typically see an argument against the possibility of intelligent extraterrestrial life based on the idea that the effects of Adam's Fall extended to the entire universe via the Adamic Dominion Mandate. This is true enough. The trouble comes when they insist that the effects of the Fall necessarily implies that intelligent extraterrestrials with a spiritual aspect would be imputed with Adam's sin nature along with the effects of the Fall which the rest of non-Adamic creation suffers under; this imputed sin nature then requires Jesus to be born and sacrificed on alien worlds for their salvation. Yet it does not follow that just because proposed intelligent aliens with a spiritual nature suffer the universal effects of the fall that they also suffer what are often termed the "spiritual effects" of the Fall (i.e., separation from God, depravity, etc.), which might be more accurately termed the "sanguine effects" of the Fall. Keep in mind that there is no remission of sin without the shedding of blood precisely because of the curse that was place upon Adam and his descendants. Christ was required to incarnate as a kinsman-redeemer to forgive the sins of Adam and cleanse his bloodline. Aliens being exempt from Adam's bloodline would be exempt from the need for salvation as much as the opportunity of salvation.

If they are unfallen, they do not need to be saved.

What If ETs are Fallen on Their Own Merit?

Of course, even if they did not fall in Adam, but fell on their own, they might need saved, but they're not really germane to the subject. If they fell in their own right and not because of Adam's sin, that is between them and their Creator; not Adam and their Creator.

For the sake of argument, we could ask whether Christ be required to be sacrificed on their world for their sins. There's no requirement here at all. However unlikely, it may be that salvation through the Earth-born Christ through future missionaries or through supernatural revelation. It may be that God offers them a totally different means of salvation, germane to the conditions of their fall. Christ could even possibly incarnate on other worlds as a God-alien as He incarnated here as a God-man. This would not, as some apologists erroneously claim, make God a polygamist. It would not give him a Terran bride, a Vulcan bride and Gungan bride, so to speak, precisely because any being saved by Christ would be incorporated into the Bride of Christ (singular).

It may be that God offers them no means of salvation at all. An appeal to equality is a fallacy based an assumed premise of equality. "If fallen aliens existed, not being of Adam's bloodline they wouldn't be able to be saved by Christ's sacrifice. Does that sound fair?" Unfortunately, the Bible answers this question in one of the most-ignored passages relevant to the terrestrial question, "What about those who've never heard of Jesus or the Gospel?" Romans 9:14-25 reminds us that God is sovereign, showing mercy on those He will and hardening the hearts of others. In this, He is not unrighteous, precisely because it is impossible to condemn the Designer for making you. God's will is based on His omniscience, and only God is wise enough to know all of these reasons. If fallen alien life existed, it would not matter whether we thought it was fair. More importantly, our perception of unfairness in no way prevents the possibility of extraterrestrial life, fallen or otherwise. Despite being intelligent and possessing a spiritual aspect, fallen angels do not seem to require or warrant salvation, nor suffer death. This implies that either being made in God's image means something other than intelligence and a spiritual nature, or that the only image bearer requiring a blood sacrifice for their sins are those who inherited the sanguine effects of Adam's Fall.

If they are fallen apart from Adam's sin, God is not required to save them.

What If ETs are Fallen as a Result of Adam's Sin?

Of course, we have to at long last consider the possibility that we discover intelligent aliens with a spiritual aspect who fell through Adam's sin. If this were the case, we must point out there isn't a single shred of Scriptural evidence that anyone outside of Adam's bloodline was imputed with the sanguine effects of the Fall. So yeah, that would be a big surprise for everyone. If it were true, much of what we said in the preceding sections holds true, except that God would certainly have to offer them the means of salvation. If Adam's sin were imputed to them, Christ's righteousness could be imputed to them as well, so it would not be necessary for Christ to incarnate on other worlds. As God did here on Earth, He could give them revelation, prophecies, and a school teacher in the form of the Law to prepare them for the Gospel. Presupposing that we encounter said extraterrestrial life, God could then either send us as missionaries with the Gospel. If we only find evidence of intelligent extraterrestrial civilization without encountering it, we could speculate that God delivered the Gospel of Christ's sacrifice for the cosmos through revelation validated by fulfilled prophecy. Incarnating on another world would be possible, possibly about as confusing for the natives as the Trinity and the idea of a God-man is to us, but feasible considering that it would still be Christ incarnate.

The only hinge is that the Bible says that Christ was sacrificed once for all. Anti-alienists tend to translate this verse as meaning "once for all men." If that's the case, then the idea of Christ incarnating on another world is really no problem. If the verse has a broader application that Christ died for all who need to be saved," then a separate incarnation of Christ on an alien world would not be necessary.

If aliens were fallen through Adam's sin and Christ died once for all who need to be saved, Christ's righteousness could be imputed to them as much as Adam's depravity was;

If aliens were fallen through Adam's sin and Christ died once for all men only, Christ could incarnate on another world and be their substitutionary atonement for the imputed (rather than sanguine) sin of Adam.

Conclusions

One last thing needs to be said. It is unlikely that we will encounter extraterrestrials fallen through Adam. The reason for this is simple: the Bible's revelation makes it pretty clear that the sanguine effects of the Fall apply only to Adam's bloodline. This is why the angels do not require or warrant salvation by Christ's incarnation and sacrifice. Angels did not fall with Adam; they fell quite apart from the Fall of Man. In fact, Lucifer's Fall predates ours. Still, it's pretty clear the sanguine effects of the Fall only apply to mankind; therefore, aliens would either be unfallen or fallen on their own merits, posing no problem for Christian theology and lacking a requirement to be saved by Christ's sacrifice. Likewise, extraterrestrial entities lacking intelligence and/or a spiritual aspect could exist within Biblical parameters, none of which would require salvation by Christ.

So can aliens be saved?

Any aliens we encounter probably won't need it. The sanguine effects of the Fall apply only to mankind. Any aliens that do requiring saving will be fallen on their own merit, meaning that their salvation is between them and their Maker, who is not obligated to save them at all or by the same means afforded to mankind. In other words, separate transaction. If it were possible to impute Adam's sin nature apart from being a member of his bloodline, then it is equally possible for the Last Adam's righteousness to be imputed to them by grace through faith.

So yeah, but it's probably not necessary.

Sapient aliens pose the only true doctrinal challenge to Christendom. Someone once pointed out that Superman is a bigger problem, doctrinally speaking, than Harry Potter! Where does Kal-El's soul go when he dies? Superman seems to possess a defined sense of morality and also a flawed nature we theologically ascribe to original sin amongst the sons of Adam; does he require salvation? How would he get saved? Did a Christ figure die for Kryptonians on their planet? Did they have a system of law, a schoolteacher like Mosaic Law, until he should receive the fullness of the Gospel here on Earth? Would God be obligated to offer salvation at all?

See the sorts of questions sapient extraterrestrials engender! A science fiction writer answers the What If questions. As Biblical Creationists we have an opportunity to use sci-fi as an exploratory apologetic to see how we might answer these scenarios based on the true revelation of God's Word.

For example, I've been working on a short story which speculates that the "locusts" of Revelation 9 are actually non-sapient aliens who hitched a ride inside a meteor called Wormwood. While Revelation 8 describes what the modern mind immediately sees as a meteor (large mountain falling from the sky) landing in the ocean, I connected the Abyss with Wormwood's crater for no other reason than I found the concept interesting. In the story, one of Wormwood's fragments lands on solid ground and the locusts awaken after the crater cools somewhat. They're a bit like brine shrimp (the bitter disappointments known as Sea Monkeys, to my fellow geeks) in that they awaken when conditions are right for life. While there is clearly a demonic element to this section of Revelation, specifically a fallen angel called Apollyon who leads the locust creatures, the locusts themselves appear to be purely physical. They are described thus in Revelation 9:1-11:

> "The fifth angel sounded his trumpet, and I saw a star that had fallen from the sky to the earth.

The star was given the key to the shaft of the Abyss. [2] When he opened the Abyss, smoke rose from it like the smoke from a gigantic furnace. The sun and sky were darkened by the smoke from the Abyss. [3] And out of the smoke locusts came down on the earth and were given power like that of scorpions of the earth. [4] They were told not to harm the grass of the earth or any plant or tree, but only those people who did not have the seal of God on their foreheads. [5] They were not allowed to kill them but only to torture them for five months. And the agony they suffered was like that of the sting of a scorpion when it strikes. [6] During those days people will seek death but will not find it; they will long to die, but death will elude them.
[7] The locusts looked like horses prepared for battle. On their heads they wore something like crowns of gold, and their faces resembled human faces. [8] Their hair was like women's hair, and their teeth were like lions' teeth. [9] They had breastplates like breastplates of iron, and the sound of their wings

was like the thundering of many horses and chariots rushing into battle. [10] They had tails with stingers, like scorpions, and in their tails they had power to torment people for five months. [11] They had as king over them the angel of the Abyss, whose name in Hebrew is Abaddon and in Greek is Apollyon (that is, Destroyer)."

So here we have a creature that stings people with a venom that doesn't kill you but makes you wish you were. And apparently the plague either lasts 5 months or the agony of a sting does. They're armored (horse prepared for battle are armored) and ugly. We would recognize them as aliens if we connected them with the meteor crash at all. It seems possible that the Revelation passage which speaks of Wormwood falling to earth and a subsequent invasion of locust creatures may speak of such non-sapient ETs. Of course, it's also possible that said locust creatures are indigenous to earth and are simply subterranean creatures we have not yet encountered. It's equally possible that they're demonic entities with physical form.

Speculations about Tribulational nightmares aside, the takeaway is that non-sapient aliens pose no threat to Christianity.

This is not a new question, by the way. Former U.S. President John Adams observed in his diary on April

24, 1756, that if many other worlds were inhabited as people then thought, then Jesus would have to die on each of those worlds:

> "Astronomers tell us, with good Reason, that not only all the Planets and Satellites in our Solar System, but all the unnumbered Worlds that revolve round the fixt Starrs are inhabited, as well as this Globe of Earth. If this is the Case all Mankind are no more in comparison of the whole rational Creation of God, than a point to the Orbit of Saturn. Perhaps all these different Ranks of Rational Beings have in a greater or less Degree, committed moral Wickedness. If so, I ask a Calvinist, whether he will subscribe to this Alternitive, "either God almighty must assume the respective shapes of all these different Species, and suffer the Penalties of their Crimes, in their Stead, or else all these Being[s]must be consigned to everlasting Perdition?""

The following day's entry comments further upon the subject:

> "The Reflection that I penned

Yesterday, appears upon the
review to be weak enough. For 1st.
we know not that the Inhabitants
of other Globes have sinned.
Nothing can be argued in this
manner, till it is proved at least
probable that all those Species of
rational Beings have revolted from
their rightful Sovereign.—When I
examine the little Prospect that lies
before me, and find an infinite
variety of Bodies in one Horizon
of perhaps two miles diameter,
how many Millions of such
Prospects there are upon the
Surface of this Earth, how many
millions of Globes there are within
our View, each of which has as
many of these prospects upon its
own surface as our Planet—great!
and marvellous are thy works!"

John Adams realized something that is very essential to the question of whether any proposed aliens would require salvation: namely, that first we would have to know whether said aliens are fallen.

You see, a sapient unfallen alien race that is subject to the fallen universe is not really a problem for Christina theology… because they don't need saved. And thus far we must admit that astrotheology has the same basic dilemma that astrobiology has: a lack of subjects.

Nevertheless, the sci-fi author in me asks the dread What If? What If we found sapient aliens who were fallen? Would they require God to come to send His Son to sacrifice themselves for their sin? Well, no. Not unless they were also made in God's image.

If they fell in their own right and not because of Adam's sin, that is between them and their Creator; not Adam and their Creator. The angelic beings who fell have not, to our knowledge, been offered a hint of salvation and no one cries foul over that! Why is not God unjust to offer them grace? The preacher in me smiles. Oh, wait. It is grace that we preach, isn't it? Doesn't the notion of grace come with the unspoken acknowledgement that God is not impugned if He does not provide a remedy for our sin; that He didn't have to do anything; that He did so out of love and mercy and for the sake of His own good Name? We do not impugn God for condemning fallen angels to hell without a mention of redemption because we know that we've no right to impugn God's justice over the matter when it is a matter of grace and grace alone that it is offered to mankind at all. It is NOT a matter of God's justice, for if we all got what we deserved, if we all got justice instead of grace, we'd be in hell tonight!

When we ask, "What about the angels? Or what about salvation for fallen aliens?" we echo Peter's question to Jesus regarding John: "Lord, what about him?" Jesus had just told Peter that he would die a martyr and Peter wanted to know if the same fate awaited John. Jesus' response was "If I want him to live until I return, what it that to you? You follow Me!"[John 21:18-22]. Like Peter, we want everything to be fair we think it should be, but God alone is sovereign and God alone is omnipotent.

Some will perhaps think I am sidestepping the issue, but I assure you I am addressing it in the only way a Biblicist should.

If aliens require salvation, will not the Lord of Heaven deal justly?

Of course, we must consider the fact that death entered the universe by Adam's sin. Yet Luke 20:36 tells us that angels do not die. There seems to be an exception to the death penalty where these created beings are concerned, and this apparent immortality of angels seems to still apply to the third of the hosts who are fallen! They are eternal in the sense that man's soul is eternal. We die physically, but heaven or hell awaits us eternally. This seems to present the solution to the dilemma: Mortality as a consequence for Adam's Fall may only apply to creatures who are, for lack of a better term, corporeal. Or perhaps the effects of the Fall only apply to denizens of this dimension of reality and not those whose natural realm is extradimensional.

I'm of the opinion that all life in this dimension is subject to the Fall's death penalty, because the Bible explicitly said that death entered into the world by man's sin [Romans 8:18-22]; therefore, we need to discuss to what extent the Fall affected any sapient aliens God may've created.

We know that they die as a result of the Fall, but do we know whether they inherited man's sin nature? Creationists tend to view both death and depravity as part and parcel to the Fall, because that is precisely the case for man. It is not the case for animals, who only die and have no sin nature. Of course, animals have been affected in other ways. Originally vegetarian creatures became carnivores or parasites, or else developed harmful and even lethal defenses. We can reasonably expect non-sapient life forms from other worlds to basically parallel what we see on Earth because the Bible says that plants and animals were cursed as a result of the Fall [Genesis 3:14, 17-18].

What of sapient life forms then? Does their cursed state make the concept of an unfallen sapient alien nothing more than a hypothetical thought exercise, but ultimately impossible? Perhaps. Animals are affected by the Fall by they are not fallen in the sense of requiring salvation. Animals do not sin; they are amoral. Nevertheless, ever since the Fall, the lion placed in a pen with a lamb does what its cursed nature compels it to do. Animals do not require salvation, so much as redemption from the corollary effects of the curse: death and corruption.

Would ET find this situation unfair? First, we have to ask if they have enough information to think it's unfair. They die. They know why? I believe so. I have no reason to believe that God would not send his angels as messengers or give them revelation of some sort. If they are unfallen and die, they would not criticize their Creator for making them subject to the penalty He placed on the creature to Whom God had given Dominion. A king falls and his kingdom suffers. A man's sin always affects more than just himself. An unfallen race would praise God for His grace and mercy in providing a means of redemption for the universe. As unfallen sapient beings, they would require no salvation. If they lack immortal souls, they would thank God for their lives, however long or brief. If they had immortal souls beyond their corporeal bodies, they would not be in danger of hell beyond death; death would simply be what it is for the Christian: a joyous reunion with their beloved Creator!

If they are not fallen, what would an encounter with them be like? Would they even want to contact us? This vein of thought offers some very interesting possibilities. David G. Johnson's *Chadash Chronicles* proposes a world that is not under the effect of original sin or God's election, a world set up as a sort of divine contest in the tradition of the testing of Job. Peter R Stone also has an interesting twist on this idea. In *A Knight from Dein*, some humans were transported to an alien world at the dispersion of Babel (so they were dispersed quite a bit further than other people groups!). Their world is both fallen and unfallen (in sections) because God created two alien species there and set them up with a Garden of Eden type test: one fell and the other didn't. There is no carnivory in the lush, unfallen lands and unsaved beings feel strong discomfort and conviction when they enter unfallen elven lands.

Neither Johnson nor Stone's scenarios negate the universal effects of the Adamic Fall; it simply notes a localized exception caused by a unique local phenomenon. Think of it this way: gravity isn't negated when a rocket leaves the planet. Rather, other forces overcome gravity at a local level, allowing gravity to be overcome for that rocket. Similarly, Christians are localized unfallen effects (sort of); we've been redeemed, even if it will take new resurrected bodies and a new heaven & earth to allow us to enjoy/realize our redeemed state. Likewise, we still have a sin nature as Christians because we inherited what I call the "spiritual genetics" of the Fall. The mind of Christ and a fallen mind war inside our heads, much as the physical alien inhabitants of Stone and Johnson's worlds war with one another.

So the question becomes: Would sapient aliens require salvation or would they merely require redemption from physical death and the other effects of the curse?

The Bible's scant revelation regarding angels may once again give us insight. We know that there was a war in heaven [Revelation 12:7-13]. We all know war is bad. Satan rebelled against God and was cast out of heaven with a third of the heavenly hosts who followed him BEFORE the Fall. The punishment God has meted out for them and the timetable He has decreed for this future judgement are completely independent matters from Adam's Fall and mankind's subsequent judgment. They knew rebellion and war before we knew sin and murder! Our punishments were not identical. Angels do not die. There is no indication that they suffer from any of the corollary effects of the Fall. They have not been given, to our knowledge, any Gospel such as mankind has been given by God's grace. It would seem then that the God who is revealed in Scripture would deal with sapient non-human races according to their own merits and situations. If angels are our example (and not some exception to a rule we're as yet ignorant of), this strongly implies that sapient races may be exempt from the corollary effects of the Fall, though they live in a universe very much cursed by the Fall of Adam. That is, if a sapient race is fallen, it is fallen on its own response to its Creator and not Adam's Fall. If this is the case, the question of sapient alien life, fallen or unfallen has no effect whatsoever on Christian doctrine.

But What IF? What If all sapient aliens were fallen along with Adam in exactly the same way mankind is? The root cause of their sin would be an imputed (as opposed to inherited) sin nature. They would sin, as all human do, because they are sinners. You see, sin is something of a spiritual computer virus. It corrupts the program and corrupts the code of everything that program produces. By analogy, we require a completely new operating system to rid ourselves of the virus, but we are completely helpless to affect that sort of change; we require the Programmer to remedy the situation. If sapient aliens were imputed the same spiritual virus we humans have, they would still be guilty of sin because they would sin according to their nature. Would they then require salvation? Yup. Would God's justice be impugned if He didn't offer it to them when they didn't commit the original sin that gave them this imputed nature? Yes and no. Scripture makes it clear that we have all sinned in Adam, yet we are also personally accountable for the sins we commit. I can't imagine aliens getting a pass on the second count. Still, God being God, we have to suppose He would give them the Gospel on account of that borrowed sin nature alone. So as in Adam all die, so in Christ all shall be made alive, right [1 Corinthians 15:22]? We need Christ to come die on an alien world, right? That's what John Adams thought. Is it true? Well, not necessarily. In fact, that seems a bit wasteful. And it may even be Scripturally prohibitive if the several passage that state that Christ died once for all includes aliens as well. Logically, the Gospel to ET would have to come from Earth or, more likely, through revelation and refer to earth and its history with Adam's Dominion and later Fall and Christ's sacrifice for sin and the resurrection as the promise of eternal life.

But wait! Don't we have to be of Adam's bloodline in order to enjoy the blessings of salvation? Isn't that why Christ came and became a man and shed His own blood for our sins? That's how it works for humanity; however, if depravity is imputed to ETs as it must be for them to be fallen in Adam (rather than on their own), then salvation may be imputed as well.

Of course, as we pointed out in an earlier chapter, there exists the probability that if aliens ever visited this planet, given the severe inconveniences of travelling across space, it would be their machines who came rather than any biological entity. Given the level of artificial intelligence required for such a mission, will we encounter sapient robots? How would we tell the real McCoy from a robot that has been convincingly programmed to mimic sapience? Or is there really any substantial difference between the two? Will sapience occur inevitably with a sufficient (but as-yet-undefined) level of complexity as evolutionists suggest? Will artificial sapience ever be valid or will the programming only be very convincing, but never authentic? How will we draw that line? What social and religious issues would that raise? What about robot rights?

These questions apply to any potentially sapient robot really, whether alien or human in origin. Assuming true artificial sapience, will androids inherent our Fallen nature as adopted children subject to the same human moral flaws (by design!) and need salvation by Christ? Or would true sapience result in robotic lifeforms that are not fallen? How would THAT impact humanity? Would they share a networked groupmind or be individuals? In a Rapture scenario, would they gain a new body? (i.e. - would they share the promise with biological believers?). What if they had no body to begin with but we only had a virtual presence but true sapience nonetheless? This field of exploratory thought is rife with possibility, especially as our concept of a "robot" or android" has come to include biological machines. Whether a mechanical man, a biological robot (simulacrum/android), a nanite cloud or a "living program" bound by the Internet, there is an as-yet-unexplored possible tie-in between Revelation 13:15 and artificial intelligence.

Food for thought, but let's get back to the aliens.

Creationist astronomer Dr. Danny Faulkner objects that "A gospel message that begins, "A long time ago in a galaxy far, far away . . ." trivializes the gospel.

To which I respond, in Appalachian, "Bullroar!" What is the difference between giving folks the Gospel today and saying, "A long, long time ago, Christ was born in a country far, far away, lived a sinless life, and died a cruel death to redeem mankind from the sin of a man who lived an even longer time ago?" What special pleading is this? Some of you have heard the tale of New Tribes Mission's efforts to reach the Mouk Tribe of Papau, New Guinea. These missionaries tried traditional evangelism methods with almost no success. In order to reach a people with absolutely no Bible knowledge, they began with two months of Old Testament Bible stories. Only after this foundation was laid did they begin teaching about Christ. After teaching them about God and the Bible, NTM missionaries taught them about "Creation, and Adam and Eve, and man's choice to sin. We explained how God promised a Savior would someday come to deliver us from sin." How is this situation substantially different than delivering the Gospel to ETs? And as I ask this, keep in mind that God may've given them revelation and perhaps even a Law to act as a schoolmaster in preparation for said Gospel [Galatians 3:24].

Skeptics may suppose that the logical consequences of sapient alien life that Jesus would have to incarnate upon and sacrifice Himself for each and every one, but this Santa Claus view of the Gospel is the product of a superficial consideration of the subject. This is true of skeptics. This is true of creationists who associate the ET question with an evolutionary worldview.

So the conclusion of the matter is this:

- Non-sapient alien life poses no threat to Christianity. Its discovery would merely confirm the notion that the Bible is a geocentric revelation to humanity.

- The possibility of unfallen sapient aliens exists because unfallen angels exist; such aliens would be affected by the curse but would not require salvation.

- Fallen sapient aliens who fell apart from Adam's fall would not necessarily receive the grace offered to mankind for salvation; God is not impugned for meting out justice rather than granting grace.

- Fallen sapient beings who fell with Adam would not require Christ to die for them on each fallen world; Christ died once for all, so if man's depravity is imputed to them, it follows that Christ's righteousness could be imputed to them as well.

The only circumstances in which alien life would truly be a problem for Christianity is if well-meaning Christians falsely conflated an absence of alien life as a prediction of the Bible.

.

15 The Truth Is Out There

My position, that we ought not to be dogmatic about the absence of extraterrestrial life when the Scriptures are silent on the subject, has generated a lot of opposition and even a little ridicule from fellow Christians. That didn't surprise me.

We're talking about the truth here, and Christians like their truth in black and white. We don't like unknowns. Christians rightly preach that the Bible should be our ultimate authority in all that it speaks. The trouble is, it doesn't really speak to the point of whether extraterrestrial life exists or not.

The Bible warns that: "He that answereth a matter before he heareth it, it is folly and shame unto him" [Proverbs 18:13]. It is equally true that he who answers with certainty before he knows for the truth for certain run the risk of inheriting that self-same shame and folly.

My point remains that, while aliens are unlikely to exist, Christians should not be dogmatic about a subject the Scriptures are themselves silent on. Almost no one seems to get that point because they're generally too busy trying to tell me that the Bible says there's no aliens.

One of the reasons that I assert that Christians ought to exercise strong caution when declaring whether aliens exist or not is because the Church is Biblically described as the pillar and ground of truth [1 Timothy 3:15]. We serve one Who is The Truth, the Way and the Life [John 14:6], by Whom came grace and truth John 1:17]. We know this. We are also oft-reminded that we are to speak the truth in love [Ephesians 4:15].

Yet some Christians are trying to support certain truth claims with bad logic, even though they tell us to watch out for such fallacies in the arguments of evolutionists. Truth is not built upon logical fallacies. We cannot be the ground and pillar of truth we're supposed to be if we build our doctrines or proposed Biblical predictions on logical fallacies. It may be that extraterrestrials do not exist; we dare not support a dogmatic view that they do not on such fallacies.

In fact, the most common objections I received could be categorized thus:

Arguments from authority. "You just need to read *Alien Intrusion.*" This is pretty much the same tactic we condemn in evolutionists when they tell us that if we'd just read a science textbook we'd finally understand evolution. My fear is that we have abandoned critical thought for the comfort of authorities. While I vigorously disagree with his assessment of Creationism, I can't help think that Roger Ebert[1] was right when he worried that:

"We may be leaving an age of irony and entering an age of credulity. In a time of shortened attention spans and instant gratification, trained by web surfing and movies with an average shot length of seconds, we absorb rather than contemplate. We want to gobble all the food on the plate, instead of considering each bite. We accept rather than select."

Arguments of irrelevant conclusions. An irrelevant conclusion is a fallacy in which someone's argument may in itself be valid, but does not address the issue in question. A prime example is the argument that the "aliens" of modern UFO sightings and alien abduction stories are likely fallen angels. This argument is in itself valid, but it doesn't address the question of whether extraterrestrial life exists at all.

Guilt by association. Polarized opposition based on the idea that aliens are an evolutionary concept or an associating belief in extraterrestrials with the UFO/alien abduction phenomenon and/or fallen angels and Satanic deception. This is also known as poisoning the well. Again, evolutionists made hold these views but that doesn't mean they are false. For example, evolutionists and creationists alike affirm adaptation, speciation, mutation and other observable biological changes. We would be fools to deny these things simply because evolutionists also affirm them. Likewise, the question of whether extraterrestrials exists is completely separate from the issue of whether aliens have visited this planet and who might be behind the UFO/alien abduction phenomenon if extraterrestrials are not involved. Saying that all aliens are fallen angels is an attempt at dismissing the big question of extraterrestrial life by giving it a negative association with the Satanic deception we suspect is involved in the idea that aliens have visited earth.

Arguments from silence. An argument from silence is a logical fallacy where someone states that something didn't happen or does not exist because the writer failed to mention it. "The Bible doesn't mention aliens, therefore aliens don't exist."

Well-meaning believers employ this fallacy when they say aliens cannot exist because the Bible doesn't mention them. In my experience, this argument from silence is, hands-down, the most common objection to extraterrestrial life by Christians on social media.

Most often, these types of arguments take the form of reductionist arguments that the Bible's anthropocentric focus excludes the possibility of extraterrestrial life. "God created the heavens and the earth for man's benefit..." This is commonly coupled with an argument from incredulity (see below). A variant of this argument is that Jesus is described as the Last Adam not the Last Vulcan. Another version is the oft-repeated comment that Jesus was incarnated as the God-man, not the God-Klingon or God-Vulcan. The doctrine that Jesus is the God-man is a necessary inference from Scripture. The fact that Scripture is silent about extraterrestrials doesn't mean that He hasn't incarnated on other worlds.

Arguments from ignorance presented as a false dilemma. An argument from ignorance is a logical fallacy where someone states that a position is true because we cannot prove it false. "We've found no evidence for extraterrestrials, therefore they do not exist."

Well-meaning Christians employ this fallacy when they claim that aliens don't exist because we, as yet, have no evidence of them. Since we can rule out alien abductions and UFO sightings as evidence of bona fide extraterrestrial life and no one has found conclusive evidence of life beyond this planet, it's true that we don't yet have evidence for alien life. This does not mean they don't exist. Remember that absence of evidence is not evidence of absence. We may yet find such evidence in the future. We've explored the tiniest fraction of the universe, thus far.

Some have claimed that I am committing my own argument from ignorance, but I'm not. I'm not even saying that aliens exist. I find it unlikely that we will even encounter any ETs that might exist, and I doubt we'll find sapient aliens at all. I am saying that we do not know that we will not eventually encounter aliens based on our present level of knowledge, and the Bible's silence on the matter precludes us from summarily ruling it out. I'm saying we cannot dogmatically say that alien life doesn't exist and that we certainly shouldn't be cocky enough to make it a prediction of the Bible that we'll never find evidence of it. I'm saying they have probably never visited Earth and we may not ever encounter them, but making "no aliens will ever be found" a prediction of the Bible based on an argument from silence and an appeal to the consequences (declaring something must be either true or false based on whether the premise leads to desirable or undesirable consequences) further based on a misapprehension of the what the theological consequences of extraterrestrial life would actually be!

Arguments from personal incredulity. "What possible purpose could God have for creating aliens on other worlds?" the existence of extraterrestrial life is not dependent upon whether or not you can figure out what God's purpose might be for creating them. I will say this, if we discover extraterrestrial life, it has a purpose [Ecclesiastes 3:1].

Appeals to equality. An appeal to equality is a fallacy based an assumed premise of equality. "If fallen aliens existed, not being of Adam's bloodline they wouldn't be able to be saved by Christ's sacrifice. Does that sound fair?" Unfortunately, the Bible answers this question in one of the most-ignored passages relevant to the terrestrial question, "What about those who've never heard of Jesus or the Gospel?" Romans 9:14-25 reminds us that God is sovereign, showing mercy on those He will and hardening the hearts of others. In this, He is not unrighteous, precisely because it is impossible to condemn the Designer for making you. God's will is based on His omniscience, and only God is wise enough to know all of these reasons. If fallen alien life existed, it would not matter whether we thought it was fair. More importantly, our perception of unfairness in no way prevents the possibility of extraterrestrial life, fallen or otherwise.

Non sequitur. Some arguments are fallacies because their conclusions do not naturally follow from the premises of the argument. We typically see an argument against the possibility of intelligent extraterrestrial life based on the idea that the effects of Adam's Fall extended to the entire universe via the Dominion Mandate. This is true enough. The trouble comes when they insist that the effects of the Fall necessarily implies that intelligent extraterrestrials with a spiritual aspect would be imputed with Adam's sin nature along with the effects of the Fall which the rest of non-Adamic creation suffers under; this imputed sin nature then requires Jesus to be born and sacrificed on alien worlds for their salvation. Yet it does not follow that just because proposed intelligent aliens with a spiritual nature suffer the universal effects of the fall that they also suffered the sanguine effects of the Fall (i.e., separation for God, depravity, etc.). Keep in mind that there is no remission of sin without the shedding of blood precisely because of the curse that was place upon Adam and his descendants. Christ was required to incarnate as a kinsman-redeemer to forgive the sins of Adam and cleanse his bloodline. Aliens being exempt from Adam's bloodline would be exempt from the need for salvation as much as the opportunity of salvation.

Arguments from special pleading. "God made man in His image, not ET." It is assumed that being made in God's image in synonymous with having a mind and a spiritual nature; some use this definition of being made in God's image to say that the Bible only records that God made man in His image, not ET (argument from silence), and that extraterrestrials with intelligence and a spiritual aspect would be impossible from a Biblical worldview. What makes this a case of special pleading is that angels are exempted from this definition. If intelligence and a spiritual nature are what is meant by being made in man's image, then angels certainly qualify as much as proposed extraterrestrials. This is significant because fallen angels do not seem to require or warrant salvation, nor suffer death. This implies that either being made in God's image means something other than intelligence and a spiritual nature, or that the only image bearer requiring a blood sacrifice for their sins are those who inherited the sanguine effects of Adam's Fall.

Quote-mining. This is a fallacy where someone quotes a passage and applies it in a manner that is out-of-context with its intended meaning. Context is important, especially when dealing with the Bible. For example, some Christians defend their anti-alien position by quoting Genesis 3:20: "And Adam called his wife's name Eve; because she was the mother of all living" and then claiming that this invalidates the idea of alien life because she lived here on Earth. Biologically speaking, Eve was only the mother of all living humans; the passages certainly doesn't imply she was the mother of all living creatures, like bees and beets and gazelles, right? So if meant literally, this verse is saying she is the mother of all living people; if meant figuratively, Eve was being called a mother of all in the sense that someone might say they are their pet's mother or in the sense that we might call her the Queen of Creation and Adam the King of Creation. In a figurative sense, Eve would still be the mother of all living things, even extraterrestrial life forms.

...

I could go on. All of these logical fallacies are committed by folks who are trying to tell us that, while the Bible is silent on the matter of extraterrestrial life, we can definitely say it does not exist based on Biblical principles. Yet these principles always seem to be propped up on bad arguments.

While I find the notion of alien life, especially the intelligent sort, to be extremely improbable, I advise caution in making dogmatic statements where the Scripture is silent. There is a vast divide between the highly improbable and the certainly impossible, and in this case it would require an act of omniscience to know with certainty that aliens do not exist. Telling folks that the Bible says what it has almost nothing to say on at all places a potential stumbling block to the Gospel if the thing we deny turns out to be true after all.

In this day and age, we all seek the certainty of a pat answer. We all want something to hang our hats on. Maybe the truest reason the Bible is silent on the subject of aliens is not that they don't exist but rather that they don't concern us.

I strongly believe that a knee-jerk rejection of the idea of alien life somewhere in the universe based on fearmongering will only serve to increase the effectiveness of the Satanic deception surrounding belief in ETs. Especially if influential creationists organizations continue to insist on creating a false dichotomy between Biblical Christianity and the possibility of alien life. Telling folks that the Bible says what it has almost nothing to say on at all places a potential stumbling block to the Gospel if the thing we deny turns out to be true after all.

They should leave the subject of aliens to science fiction authors like myself rather than making dogmatic statements about something the Bible doesn't clearly address. Because God may not limit our horizons to keep those inferred doctrines from being falsified.

***

Notes

1. Ebert, Roger. "This Is the Dawning of the Age of credulity." RogerEbert.com. September 23, 2008. Web. Retrieved October 15, 2015.

ABOUT THE AUTHOR

Tony Breeden is an author, illustrator, creation speaker, apologist and Gospel preacher from West Virginia. He is the founder of DefGen.org, CreationLetter.com and CreationSundays.com. He got the writing bug as a child when his late aunt Sharon helped him make his very first book about dinosaurs, vigorously illustrated in crayon.

His first book, Johnny Came Home, was published September 28, 2012.

You can find out more about the author and his books at TonyBreedenBooks.com. You can find him on Facebook at Facebook.com/tonybreedenbooks.

Also by Tony Breeden

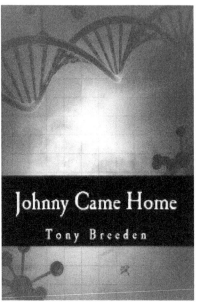

Three years after the fire that took his home and his family, John Lazarus returns to the town of Midwich searching for answers to why he can do extraordinary things no one's ever seen outside of a comic book. Is he human? Alien? Something more? The answers lie within Titan BioTech, mysterious complex that overshadows Midwich. But someone else wants Titan's secrets too and will stop at nothing to make sure that she alone possesses them.

What would a world of men and women with superpowers mean for humanity? Would they represent the next stage of human evolution? Or might there be a different explanation?

Three years ago, John Lazarus left Midwich, vowing never to return. But today... ***Johnny Came Home.***

Made in the USA
Coppell, TX
15 December 2021